D0874142

DISEASES & DISORDERS

Plague

Lizabeth Hardman

LUCENT BOOKS
A part of Gale, Cengage Learning

GALE
CENGAGE Learning

Detroit • New York • San Francisco • New Haven, Conn • Waterville, Maine • London

GALE
CENGAGE Learning

LIBRARY OF CONGRESS CATALOGING-IN-PUBLICATION DATA

Hardman, Lizabeth.
  Plague / by Lizabeth Hardman.
    p. cm. -- (Diseases and disorders)
  Includes bibliographical references and index.
  ISBN 978-1-4205-0145-2 (hardcover)
  1. Plague--Juvenile literature. I. Title.
  RC171.H37 2009
  616.9'232--dc22
                                                    2009011001

Lucent Books
27500 Drake Rd.
Farmington Hills, MI 48331

ISBN-13: 978-1-4205-0145-2
ISBN-10: 1-4205-0145-3

Printed in the United States of America
1 2 3 4 5 6 7 13 12 11 10 09

Table of Contents

"The Most Difficult Puzzles Ever Devised"

Charles Best, one of the pioneers in the search for a cure for diabetes, once explained what it is about medical research that intrigued him so. "It's not just the gratification of knowing one is helping people," he confided, "although that probably is a more heroic and selfless motivation. Those feelings may enter in, but truly, what I find best is the feeling of going toe to toe with nature, of trying to solve the most difficult puzzles ever devised. The answers are there somewhere, those keys that will solve the puzzle and make the patient well. But how will those keys be found?"

Since the dawn of civilization, nothing has so puzzled people—and often frightened them, as well—as the onset of illness in a body or mind that had seemed healthy before. A seizure, the inability of a heart to pump, the sudden deterioration of muscle tone in a small child—being unable to reverse such conditions or even to understand why they occur was unspeakably frustrating to healers. Even before there were names for such conditions, even before they were understood at all, each was a reminder of how complex the human body was, and how vulnerable.

While our grappling with understanding diseases has been frustrating at times, it has also provided some of humankind's most heroic accomplishments. Alexander Fleming's accidental discovery in 1928 of a mold that could be turned into penicillin has resulted in the saving of untold millions of lives. The isolation of the enzyme insulin has reversed what was once a death sentence for anyone with diabetes. There have been great strides in combating conditions for which there is not yet a cure, too. Medicines can help AIDS patients live longer, diagnostic tools such as mammography and ultrasounds can help doctors find tumors while they are treatable, and laser surgery techniques have made the most intricate, minute operations routine.

This "toe-to-toe" competition with diseases and disorders is even more remarkable when seen in a historical continuum. An astonishing amount of progress has been made in a very short time. Just two hundred years ago, the existence of germs as a cause of some diseases was unknown. In fact, it was less than 150 years ago that a British surgeon named Joseph Lister had difficulty persuading his fellow doctors that washing their hands before delivering a baby might increase the chances of a healthy delivery (especially if they had just attended to a diseased patient)!

Each book in Lucent's Diseases and Disorders series explores a disease or disorder and the knowledge that has been accumulated (or discarded) by doctors through the years. Each book also examines the tools used for pinpointing a diagnosis, as well as the various means that are used to treat or cure a disease. Finally, new ideas are presented—techniques or medicines that may be on the horizon.

Frustration and disappointment are still part of medicine, for not every disease or condition can be cured or prevented. But the limitations of knowledge are being pushed outward constantly; the "most difficult puzzles ever devised" are finding challengers every day.

The Scourge of Mankind

The tombstone, dated 1437, stands in the churchyard of St. John's Church in Nuremberg, Germany. The inscription on it hints at a terrible tragedy that has taken place there:

> Was that not sad and painful to relate,
> I died with thirteen of my family on the same date?

Such was the effect of a devastating pestilence that had swept through not only the city of Nuremberg but almost all of Europe and much of Asia as well, starting a hundred years earlier. Because it was thought to be a punishment from God, it was called "plague," from the Latin *plaga*, meaning a blow or wound inflicted by a god. By the time the last of several waves of the disease had ended, the Great Mortality, or the "Black Death," as the terrifying illness came to be called in the nineteenth century, had wiped out approximately 43 million people worldwide—20 to 30 million in Europe alone, almost half of its total population at the time.

In his book *The Great Mortality*, John Kelly, an expert in European history, calls the fourteenth-century plague "the greatest natural disaster in human history."[1] Historian Norman F. Cantor agrees. "The Black Death of 1348–49 was the greatest biomedical disaster in European and possibly world history," he says. "The so-called Spanish influenza epidemic of 1918 killed possibly fifty million people worldwide. But the mortality rate in proportion to total population was obviously relatively small compared to the impact of the Black Death—between 30 percent and 50 percent of Europe's population."[2]

As devastating as the Black Death of the Middle Ages was, it was not the only pandemic, or worldwide outbreak, of plague. In recorded history, three such pandemics of the disease have been described. The first, called the Plague of Justinian, happened in the sixth century and swept from Egypt west to Britain and east as far as China. It killed an estimated 100 million people and is thought to mark the beginning of the Dark Ages. The Black Death of the 1300s was the second to occur. The third pandemic began in China in 1892 and spread to many parts of the world, including the United States.

This fourteenth-century painting by Giuseppe Sabatelli depicts the Black Death in Florence, Italy.

Society Changed Forever

All three pandemics had significant and lasting impacts on human society. After the Plague of Justinian and the Black Death, the enormous loss of life led to a sharp decline in the population. Both pandemics caused a severe labor shortage, and the peasants who were left found themselves and their skills much more valuable. Peasants in both eras began to demand higher wages and more freedom from their masters, and in 1381 English peasants staged a revolt against them. Attitudes about religion, medical practice, and personal hygiene were forever altered by the experience. Writes historian Cantor:

> The pestilence deeply affected individual and family behavior and consciousness. It put severe strains on the social, political, and economic systems. It threatened the stability and viability of civilization. It was as if a neutron bomb had been detonated. Nothing like this had ever happened before or since in the recorded history of mankind, and the men and women of the fourteenth century would never be the same.[3]

During and after the third pandemic, the courageous scientists and doctors who were sent to the Far East to fight it added a great deal of valuable knowledge about plague and other diseases.

The Plague Today

Plague is a very old disease that will likely always be present. In many parts of the world, plague is endemic—it is present to some degree all the time. Unlike smallpox, scientists do not believe that plague can be eradicated, or completely eliminated from existence, because it lives in the bodies of millions of animals and in the fleas that spread it in many parts of the world. Today, about one thousand to two thousand cases of plague are reported worldwide each year. Larger outbreaks occur occasionally in Asia, Africa, and South America. They

Cases of pneumonic plague were reported in 1994 in Surat, India, where there are poor sanitary conditions and high rodent populations.

can happen in rural areas, but most often they occur in poorer urban areas with overcrowded, unsanitary conditions and a high rodent population.

No cases of plague have been reported in Europe since World War II, and it does not exist at all in Australia. In the United States, about ten to twenty cases are reported each year, most of them in the southwestern states, where plague is endemic. Most cases in the United States are caused by bites from infected prairie dogs, and even with today's effective antibiotics, about 14 percent of these patients die. Although one especially severe form of plague can be spread directly from person to person, no occurrence of this has been reported in the United States since 1924.

Over the centuries, the word "plague" has come to mean any kind of devastating or frightening illness or catastrophe, and the word alone still has the ability to spark a certain amount of fear and anxiety in many people. Throughout history, plague has been blamed for the deaths of nearly 200 million people. Today, however, despite the occasional outbreak, plague no longer sweeps through entire civilizations as it did long ago, leaving death and destruction in its wake. Improved sanitation, better public health programs and education, effective medicines to treat plague, and a much better understanding about what plague is and how it works make another plague pandemic very unlikely.

CHAPTER ONE

What Is Plague?

Plague is a very serious, highly virulent (meaning it causes a great deal of damage to the body), often fatal disease that is caused by a microscopic organism called a bacterium. Bacteria are one of several types of organisms that can cause diseases. Other organisms that can cause diseases include viruses, fungi, and parasites. Organisms that cause diseases are called pathogens, also commonly called germs.

The plague bacterium is found mainly in rodents, especially rats, and lives in the gut of the fleas that feed on them. Plague is spread when an animal or human is bitten either by the rodent or the flea that carries the plague bacterium in its body. One form of plague, called pneumonic plague, can also be spread directly from person to person by coughing or sneezing. Because plague can be spread from one animal or human to another, it is called an infectious disease.

Infectious Diseases

Infectious diseases are caused by pathogens that invade, or infect, other living organisms, cause illness in them, and can be spread to other living organisms. Pathogens can infect people in several different ways. They can pass through the air on tiny water droplets and may be inhaled through regular breathing. They can get into the body through eating or drinking contaminated food or water, or through cuts in the skin. They can be transferred by direct physical contact between people, or they can be introduced into the body by

Rodents, such as rats, can be hosts to plague-infected fleas.

insects that bite an infected animal and then bite a healthy animal or person.

Insects such as fleas that transfer a pathogen from one animal or person to another are called disease vectors. Malaria, carried by mosquitoes, is an example of a vector-borne human disease. Plague is also a vector-borne disease that affects both animals and humans. The vector is the flea. The animal that the flea lives on is called the host animal. Plague needs a bite from an infected host animal or its fleas in order to get into the bloodstream and infect another animal or person. Over two hundred different species of mammals can carry plague organisms in their bodies and possibly spread it to humans, but animals that carry a disease in a very large part of their population are called reservoirs for that disease. Rodents such as rats and marmots (large rodents similar to woodchucks) are natural reservoirs for the plague pathogen, a bacterium called *Yersinia pestis*, abbreviated *Y. pestis*.

Studying Diseases: Epidemiology

Epidemiology is the study of disease and illness in humans and animals. Those who practice it are called epidemiologists. Epidemiologists study many different factors that affect the health or illness of a population. They try to identify risk factors that make it more likely that a person will get a particular illness, and what factors help protect against illness. For example, in 1954 British epidemiologists presented evidence of the strong link between cigarette smoking and lung cancer. They learn about possible causes of disease, how diseases spread, and how they can be controlled. Many epidemiologists are physicians, but many are trained in other health-related fields such as public health or nursing. Researchers in epidemiology may look at disease outbreaks that have already occurred to discover how they happened, or they may study the potential for future outbreaks in order to minimize or prevent them from happening in the first place. The information learned by epidemiologists is valuable in developing public health programs that educate people about their health.

Epidemiology was originally developed to learn about infectious diseases like smallpox, malaria, cholera, or plague, but today it also includes noncommunicable diseases like cancer and heart disease, as well as illnesses caused by environmental factors. The Greek physician Hippocrates is sometimes called the father of epidemiology because he was the first to write about how environment affects health and illness. He coined the words "endemic" and "epidemic." Today's epidemiologists might work "in the field"—out in the community—or they may work for private organizations, hospitals, universities, or government agencies.

The Plague Germ: *Yersinia Pestis*

Yersinia pestis is one of a group of bacteria in the *Yersinia* family. *Yersinia* bacteria are shaped like tiny rods. Rod-shaped bacteria are called bacilli. Most *Yersinia* bacteria are fairly harmless, causing a mild form of stomach ailment, but *Y. pestis* causes the dreaded and potentially fatal plague.

Yersinia bacteria have not always been able to cause the plague. In 2002 researchers discovered that a change in a single gene of an ancestor of *Y. pestis* allowed the bacterium to survive in the gut of fleas. From there, according to scientists at the National Institutes of Health,

> the bacterium gradually changed from a germ that causes a mild human stomach illness acquired via food or water to the flea-borne agent of the "Black Death." The gene change allowed the bacteria to be transmitted through the bite of an insect—in this case, the flea—an adaptation that distinguishes *Yersinia pestis* from all closely related, more benign [harmless] gut bacteria.[4]

It is not uncommon for viruses and bacteria to change their own genetics in order to adapt to new environments and improve their chances of survival. Says plague investigator B. Joseph Hinnebusch, the leader of the 2002 study, "Our research illustrates how a single genetic change can profoundly affect the evolution of disease. In this case, that genetic change set the stage for a completely new route of disease transmission."[5] Two years later, researchers comparing the genetics of *Y. pestis* and another *Yersinia* species found that *Y. pestis* actually lacks 317 genes that the other species still has. The researchers believe that the loss of those genes caused *Y. pestis* to become more dangerous than its relatives and more suited to living and multiplying in the flea gut. These important genetic changes explain how plague is so easily spread from rodent to human.

How Plague Is Spread

Plague can be transmitted to humans in several ways, but the most common is by way of the flea in which it lives.

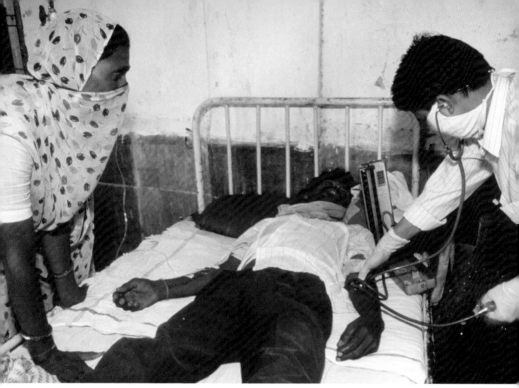

A victim of India's pneumonic plague gets treatment in a hospital. This form of plague is transferred from person to person by coughing or sneezing.

When the flea bites an infected host rodent, the bacterium settles in the gut of the flea and begins to multiply there. Eventually, so many bacteria build up that the flea's gut becomes blocked. If the flea then tries to feed on an uninfected rodent, it regurgitates the infected blood into the new host rodent. The disease is fatal to the rodent, so when it finally dies, the flea must find a new source of food. If the flea happens to land on and bite a person, the infected blood is regurgitated into the person, who then becomes infected with the plague organism.

A person can also get plague by being bitten by an infected rodent, but this is less common. It can also be transmitted by handling animals that have died from plague, if their blood gets into the person's body through a cut or other break in the skin. It is also possible for domestic dogs and cats that have had contact with plague-infested wild rodents to transmit plague to their owners, either directly or by carrying infected fleas into the house. One very severe form of plague, called pneumonic

Plague in Other Animals

In July 2005 a pet cat in southern Wyoming was diagnosed with bubonic plague. It was the fourth cat diagnosed that year—an unusual occurrence for that part of the country. Health officials knew that rodent populations in Wyoming were up that year, and they believe the cats were infected by catching infected rodents.

Plague is not common in animals other than rodents, but it has been reported in cats, mountain lions, bobcats, goats, camels, mule deer, pronghorn antelope, and at least one llama. Dogs can get it, too, but are less likely actually to develop symptoms. Symptoms in cats and dogs are similar to the human illness—fever, loss of appetite, extreme fatigue, and enlarged lymph nodes, or buboes. They may also have mouth sores, skin abscesses, eye discharge, vomiting, and diarrhea. The bubonic form of plague is most common, but cats can also develop septicemic plague, with high heart rate, weak pulse, bleeding, and respiratory distress. They can also get secondary pneumonic plague, with cough and other breathing problems and organ failure. Methods of diagnosis and treatment are very similar to that for humans.

The main concern when domestic animals get the plague is the increased risk of transmission to humans. Dogs and cats can bring plague-infected fleas into the house, or they can transmit it directly to people who handle them, especially if the animal has a cough. Rodent and flea control are the most important parts of plague prevention in domestic animals.

plague, can be transmitted from person to person by coughing or sneezing. As with any infection, when the plague organism gets into the body, it triggers the immune system to go to work.

The Immune System

The human immune system is a very complex system of special cells, organs, and tissues that help fight infections and keep people healthy. These organs, cells, and tissues have the ability to communicate with each other so that the immune system can produce the right kind of response for the particular problem, whether it is a bacterium or a splinter or a cut in the skin. Signs and symptoms such as fever, skin redness, swelling, and the presence of pus are signs that the immune system is working.

Any foreign item that gets into the body and is not recognized by the immune system as a normal part of the body is called an antigen. When an antigen, such as a pathogen, gets into the body, the immune system responds by sending specialized cells called leukocytes to hunt down and destroy the antigen. Leukocytes are made in several places in the body—in the bone marrow, the spleen, and the thymus gland. They come in two types—T cells and B cells. T cells directly attack antigens and destroy them. "T" stands for the thymus gland, where T cells mature. B cells produce antibodies, special proteins that attach to an antigen and make it easier for the T cells to destroy them. "B" refers to the bone marrow, where they mature.

The lymphatic system is the part of the immune system responsible for producing and storing leukocytes and for transporting them to the site of the infection. The leukocytes travel to wherever they are needed through tiny vessels, called lymphatic vessels, which run roughly alongside the blood vessels. They are stored in small structures called lymph nodes, located throughout the body and in clusters in areas such as the neck, armpits, and groin. The lymph nodes of a person who gets an infection may become swollen and somewhat painful, as more leukocytes are manufactured to fight the infection.

Plague and the Immune System

The reason that plague is so virulent is because of the way it affects the immune system. It is very difficult for the human immune system to get rid of *Y. pestis*, for two main reasons. First, once it enters the body it forms a thick protective layer around itself that shields it from leukocytes and other immune system defense mechanisms. This protective layer can be formed only if the organism's body temperature is at least 98 degrees Fahrenheit (37.5 degrees Celsius), which is within the normal range for humans and most other mammals.

Second, the plague bacterium also has the ability to cut off communication between immune system cells by interfering with the cell molecules that are necessary for the communication to take place. "*Yersinia pestis* is a clever pathogen," says one of the researchers who helped discover this ability. "It found our Achilles heel [weak spot]—one family of molecules used by every mammalian cell to transmit signals involved in the immune response."[6] Without this communica-

The bacterium that causes the bubonic plague attacks the immune system, multiplies, and virtually takes over other organs.

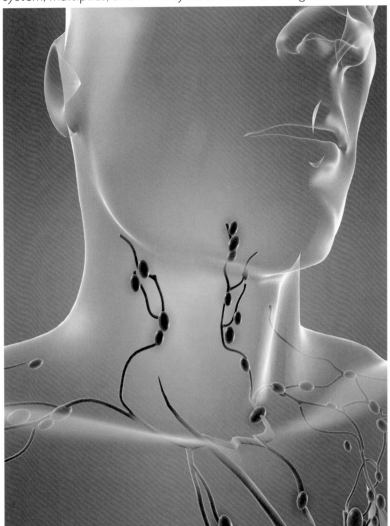

tion, the immune system cannot fight the invasion effectively. The bacteria have time to travel through the bloodstream to other organs, especially the lungs, spleen, liver, and kidneys, where they multiply to enormous numbers, completely take over the organ, and replace its tissues with colonies of its own. This leads to the eventual death of the infected animal or person.

Plague is caused by only one organism, *Y. pestis*, but it exists in three different forms, each with its own set of symptoms. The three kinds are called bubonic plague, septicemic plague, and pneumonic plague.

Bubonic Plague

Of the three kinds of plague, the most common and well known is bubonic plague. Bubonic plague (along with the pneumonic form) is blamed for causing the Black Death of the fourteenth century.

Symptoms of bubonic plague usually appear suddenly, within two to five days after the bite of the flea. Early symptoms include fever and chills (signs of the immune response), severe headache, sore throat, and muscle aches. Later on, vomiting, diarrhea, seizures, and respiratory failure may occur.

The bacteria attack the immune system quickly and travel through the lymphatic vessels until they reach a group of lymph nodes. In response to the infection, the nodes become inflamed, swollen, warm to the touch, and very painful. These swollen nodes are known as buboes (from the Greek word for groin, *boubon*), and they are what give the disease its name. Buboes are most commonly seen in the groin, the neck, or in the armpits, depending on the location of the flea bite. They can grow to be as large as an egg.

With treatment, bubonic plague causes death in 1 to 15 percent of its victims, and in 40 to 60 percent of its victims if it goes untreated. If it gets into the bloodstream, it can cause the second form of plague—the very dangerous septicemic plague, also called plague septicemia.

Septicemic Plague

Septicemia is an infection of the blood, and septicemic plague is an infection of the bloodstream with the plague organism. Plague septicemia can be a symptom of bubonic plague, or it can develop by itself directly from the flea bite. Symptoms of septicemic plague can start very quickly if the flea bite is near the mouth or throat. Buboes may be present if it develops as a symptom of bubonic plague. Other symptoms of this form of plague include high fever, abdominal pain with diarrhea and vomiting, bleeding from the mouth, nose, or rectum, and septic shock, a sudden, life-threatening loss of blood pressure caused by overwhelming infection. A very serious symptom of septicemic plague is gangrene, caused by the destruction and blockage of blood vessels because of the blood infection. Gangrene causes the tissues to die and eventually turn black. It happens most commonly in areas where the vessels are smaller, such as the hands and fingers, feet and toes, and nose. The blackening of the skin is what gave the plague the nickname "Black Death."

A very serious symptom of septicemic plague is gangrene (pictured), which is caused by the destruction and blockage of blood vessels due to infection.

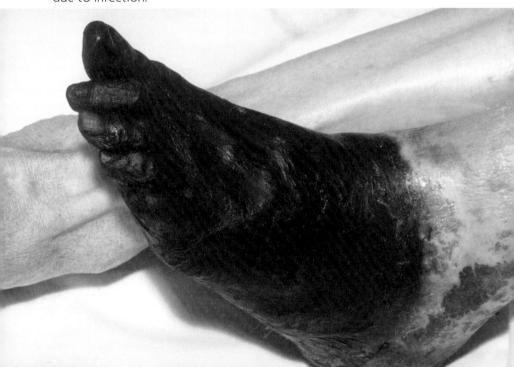

Septicemic plague is often misdiagnosed because it may not show the characteristic buboes and because septicemia can be caused by many different kinds of infections. For this reason, it has a higher mortality rate than bubonic plague, about 40 percent in treated cases. Without treatment, it is always fatal.

Pneumonic Plague

On August 22, 1992, a thirty-one-year-old man from Tucson, Arizona, became ill with abdominal cramps two days after returning home from a friend's house in Colorado. The next day he developed fever, nausea, vomiting, diarrhea, and cough. On August 25 he went into the hospital in septic shock. He was given antibiotics to fight the infection, but it was already too late. He died the next day, four days after he first became sick. After he died, an examination of his body tissues revealed that he had died of pneumonic plague.

The word *pneumonic* means related to the lungs. Pneumonic plague, or plague pneumonia, is the least common of the three types of plague, but it is also the most dangerous. Pneumonic plague is the only one of the three that does not need a bite from an animal or flea to spread it. It is spread by inhaling infected droplets from a sneeze or a cough from an infected animal or person. Like septicemic plague, pneumonic plague can also develop as a complication of one of the other two kinds of plague.

Symptoms start within a day or two of breathing the infected droplets. Early signs include severe headache, nausea, vomiting, and fatigue. The symptoms worsen very quickly to include high fever, difficulty breathing, and coughing up blood. The infection soon overwhelms the body's defenses, and the patient dies from respiratory failure and loss of blood. Pneumonic plague is so dangerous because it must be diagnosed and treated within a day of the start of symptoms. Even with treatment, more than half of its victims die, often before it is even diagnosed. Like septicemic plague, if it is not treated, it is always fatal.

A diagnosis of pneumonic plague is considered a public health emergency because it can be spread so easily from person to person, and because its symptoms progress so rapidly. It is one of the possible reasons for the rapid spread of the Black Death in the fourteenth century. Although cases are still reported in the United States, animals are the source of infection. No cases of pneumonic plague are known to have been spread directly from one human to another since 1924.

Diagnosing Plague

Because of the rapid progression of symptoms and the high mortality rate if it is not treated, diagnosing plague quickly and accurately is important. The first step is to get an accurate account of the symptoms—what they are and when they started. In the case of bubonic plague, the large, swollen, and painful buboes are an obvious finding and may lead the doctor to suspect plague, especially if the patient lives in an area where plague is endemic, and especially if the swollen nodes are accompanied by fever, chills, and extreme fatigue. Painful lymph nodes can be caused by many different things, however, so the doctor will want to get a complete health history from the patient, including past illnesses. If plague is a possibility, the doctor will ask more specific questions about the patient's whereabouts and activities in the last few days, and if he or she has been in contact with rodents of any kind or with any sick animals.

Because most of the symptoms of plague suggest an infection of some kind, the doctor will likely take samples of the patient's blood, urine, and any sputum, or substance that may be coughed up. Also, fluid or pus may be drawn out of a bubo using a needle and a syringe. The samples are examined under the microscope to see if plague organisms are present, and cultures are done to see if organisms can be grown in the laboratory from the samples. Laboratory cultures provide more of an organism to examine, thereby making the diagnosis more accurate. They also give doctors a supply of organisms on which to test different antibiotics to see which will be the most effective. Cultures can take up to forty-eight hours to yield results, so until the cause of the infection is identified, the patient must be isolated in a separate room, and health care providers must

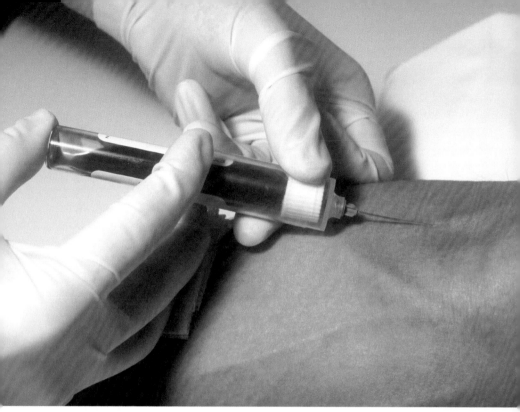

A doctor who suspects that a patient is infected with the plague will order blood samples for analysis to determine if the patient is infected.

protect themselves by wearing gowns, gloves, eye shields, and masks whenever they go into that room.

If the cultures confirm a diagnosis of plague, a specialist in infectious disease will be brought in for counsel. Because plague is so rare in the United States, and because it is so dangerous, the case will be reported to the local health department and to the Centers for Disease Control and Prevention in Atlanta, Georgia. These health officials will do more extensive investigating to find out how and where the patient contracted plague so that a potential outbreak can be prevented.

Treating Plague

Treating plague quickly is so important that doctors will not wait for the cultures to be completed before starting. Treatment starts as soon as plague is even suspected, based on the symptoms and the patient's recent activities. The first line of plague treatment, as with any bacterial infection, is with antibiotics. Antibiotics are drugs that prevent or stop an infection caused by bacteria. They are not effective for infections caused by viruses or other pathogens.

The best antibiotic for treating plague is called streptomycin. Streptomycin works by interfering with the bacterium's ability to make proteins that are necessary for its survival. It also damages the bacterium's cell membrane, which makes it easier for the antibiotic to get into the cell. Streptomycin is given either intravenously (injections into a vein) or intramuscularly (injections into a muscle) for ten days, or until the patient's temperature has stayed normal for three days. Streptomycin has some potentially serious side effects, however. It can be harmful to cells in the middle and inner ear and in the kidneys and can damage these organs. For this reason, another antibiotic called gentamicin can also be used to treat plague. Some other antibiotics can be used as well, but they are generally not as effective as streptomycin and gentamicin.

Even when antibiotic treatment is started promptly, plague may still cause very serious complications because it progresses so fast. Septic shock with multiple organ failure is a potentially life-threatening complication of plague that requires more intensive, specialized treatments.

Septic Shock

Septic shock is caused by overwhelming infection in the blood that the immune system cannot handle. In septic shock, toxins—harmful chemicals produced by the bacteria—cause the blood vessels to dilate, or widen. This causes the blood pressure to drop very low, and vital organs such as the kidneys and brain are deprived of an adequate blood supply. The heart tries to make up for this by pumping harder, but eventually the toxins and the work overload weaken the heart. This further deprives the vital organs of their blood supply. Tissues that lack adequate blood supply release a chemical called lactic acid into the blood. Acidic blood causes many other organs to fail.

Septic shock can lead to a life-threatening situation called multiple organ failure.

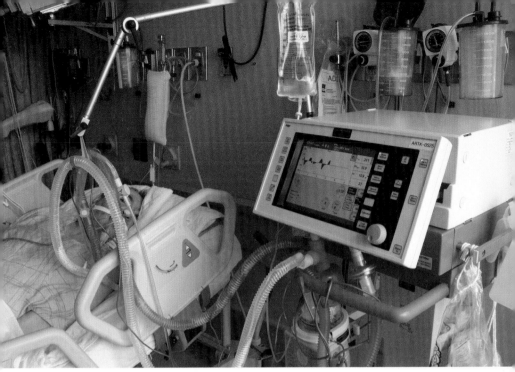

Septic shock can lead to multiple organ failure, requiring the patient to be admitted to the intensive care unit of a hospital, where fluids are given intravenously and machines are used to keep the patient alive.

Multiple organ failure is just what it sounds like—the malfunction and eventual failure of the body's organs, especially the kidneys, heart, and lungs. When the kidneys fail, they stop making urine, and toxic waste products build up in the blood. When the heart fails, fluids build up in the tissues, causing generalized swelling, and the other organs do not get enough oxygen. Fluid also builds up in the lungs, and the patient cannot breathe, a condition called acute respiratory distress syndrome (ARDS).

The patient in septic shock must be admitted to the intensive care unit for close monitoring. Antibiotics are continued to fight the infection. Special drugs and large amounts of intravenous (IV) fluids are given to support the blood pressure. Extra oxygen is given to help support the vital organs. If the patient can no longer breathe adequately, he or she will need to be put on a ventilator. In spite of all these efforts, about 25 percent of patients in septic shock die. Septic shock with multiple organ failure is what leads to death in the plague patient.

CHAPTER TWO

The Plague in Ancient Times

Plague has been known to people since very ancient times. Some scholars believe that references to widespread illnesses in the Old Testament of the Bible are referring to the plague. One of the earliest records of plague was written by Greek physician Rufus of Ephesus, who lived in the first century A.D. An outbreak of plague had occurred in the Middle East. Rufus wrote, "The buboes that are called pestilential, are very acute and very fatal, especially those which . . . they say were accompanied by high fever, agonizing pain, severe constitutional disturbance, delirium, and the appearance of large, hard buboes that did not suppurate [discharge pus], not only in the usual regions of the body, but also at the back of the knee and in the bend of the elbow, where, as a rule, similar fevers do not cause their formation."[7]

Although the existence of plague was well known to most ancient people, it was mostly a disease of rats and other rodents. Outbreaks in humans happened occasionally, but the first true pandemic—an extreme outbreak of disease that spreads to many countries—happened in the middle of the sixth century A.D. and lasted for almost fifty years. The first pandemic is often called "Justinian's Plague," or "the Plague of Justinian," because it happened during the reign of the emperor Justinian, who ruled most of the known world in the sixth century.

The World of the Sixth Century

By the third century A.D., the lands ruled by the Roman Empire had become so widespread that it was almost impossible for the leaders in Rome to manage all their territories effectively. In A.D. 285 the Roman emperor Diocletian divided the empire into two parts—the eastern empire and the western empire. Rome remained the capital of the western empire. The capital of the eastern empire was Nicomedia, in what is now Turkey. In A.D. 324, the emperor Constantine, the first Christian emperor, moved the eastern capital to the city of Byzantium, which he renamed Constantinople, after himself. Today, the city is called Istanbul.

The first pandemic is often called "Justinian's Plague" because it happened during the reign of Byzantine emperor Justinian in the sixth century.

The Mystery of the Athenian Plague

One of the earliest documented outbreaks of a disease long thought to be plague is commonly known as the Athenian plague. This outbreak lasted from 430 B.C. until 426 B.C. It was thought to have started in Ethiopa, an African country. From there it spread throughout Egypt and into Greece. In those days, Greece was not a unified country but a collection of independent city-states. The disease outbreak occurred during the Peloponnesian Wars, fought between two of these city-states—Athens and Sparta.

The main source of information about the Athenian plague comes from the writings of Thucydides, a historian and general in the Athenian army, who caught the disease himself but lived to write about it. His very detailed description included symptoms such as headaches, rashes, fever, coughing up blood, stomach cramps, and vomiting. Most victims died on the seventh or eighth day. Because he did not describe actual buboes, some question has always existed among historians as to whether or not the disease was actually the plague or something else.

In 1994 archeologists from the University of Athens discovered a mass grave containing about 150 bodies. The remains were dated to about the same time as the Athenian plague, so the scientists thought they might be from some of its victims. The researchers collected three teeth from the remains and extracted the dental pulp—the soft material under the hard enamel layer. Dental pulp can retain microbes for centuries at a time. They tested the pulp for several diseases, including plague, but found a match with the bacterium that causes typhoid fever. The symptoms of typhoid, which is spread through contaminated food and water, are very similar to those described by Thucydides. In this way, scientists were finally able to close the case of the mysterious "Athenian plague."

By the early 400s the western empire had been overrun and conquered by tribes from Asia, led by Attila the Hun, and Germanic tribes from the north. The eastern part was ruled by a succession of emperors and later became known as the Byzantine Empire. The Byzantine Empire was very different from the old Roman Empire. Greek was the main language spoken, rather than Latin. Byzantine culture and traditions were a blend of Greek, Roman, European, and, later, Islamic cultures. The break from the Roman past was made complete during the reign of the emperor Justinian.

Justinian

The emperor Justinian ruled the Byzantine Empire from 527 until his death in 565. Although he was born into a peasant family, he was adopted as a child by his uncle Justin, who named him. Justin was a member of the Imperial Guard and became emperor in 518. When Justin died, Justinian became the new emperor.

Justinian was not a very good soldier, but he was a brilliant statesman and diplomat who had a grand vision for the future of his empire. He had the ability to win over his enemies without going to war, by educating them, giving them land, converting them to Christianity when he could, and even finding them wives.

Justinian is noted for several important accomplishments that helped make the Byzantine Empire very different from the western Roman Empire. He completely rewrote the old Roman codes of law, part of it in Greek. This law, called the *Corpus Juris Civilis* (Latin, meaning *Body of Civil Law*), is the basis for codes of law even today. He contributed greatly to developing Byzantine culture and architecture. One of the world's most beautiful and famous churches, the Hagia Sophia, was built during his reign.

One of Justinian's major goals was to reunite the eastern and western empires and make them one again, with himself as the only emperor. While not a warrior himself, he was an excellent military ruler, and under his rule, most of the lands of the western empire around the Mediterranean Sea, including the city

Justinian contributed greatly to developing Byzantine culture and architecture. One of the world's most beautiful and famous churches, the Hagia Sophia, was built during his reign.

of Rome, were recovered from the Germanic tribes that had taken them in the previous century. Under Justinian, the Byzantine Empire grew and flourished until the year 542, when the mighty empire was brought down by one of the tiniest of living things—the deadly *Yersinia pestis* bacterium. By the time the pandemic ended, it had claimed the lives of about 100 million people—half of the population of the known world. The physicians of the time were helpless to do anything but stand by and watch the devastation.

Medicine in the Sixth Century

At the time of Justinian's reign, medical knowledge was taken mostly from ancient Greek and Roman knowledge, contributed by philosopher-physicians such as Galen and Hippocrates. Illness was thought to be caused by an imbalance of bodily fluids—the four "humors." The humors were black bile, yellow bile, phlegm, and blood. The humors were produced by different organs in the body, and an imbalance in the humors caused illness in the part of the body where they were produced. Diagnosis of disease was largely done by examining the body's fluids, especially the urine. A person could keep his or her humors in balance with proper diet, adequate sleep, good hygiene, medicines and herbs, and bloodletting—opening a vein to release blood in an attempt to restore balance of the humors. Ideas about the causes and cures of illnesses were a mixture of science, magic, and spiritual thinking, with concepts such as destiny, sin, and astrology considered as important as physical causes. Little was known about anatomy, as laws forbade dissection of corpses, and only a very few surgical treatments were available. When it came to treating or preventing large-scale epidemics of disease such as the plague, doctors could do very little.

Justinian's Plague

Most of what is known about this first pandemic of plague comes from three sources. One of them, the work of John of Ephesus, exists only in fragments. The second is the work of lawyer and historian Evagrius Scholasticus, who wrote a historical account about the years 431 to 594. It includes his observations about the plague, including details of his own personal experience with it:

> [The plague] took its rise from Aethiopia [a country in eastern Africa] . . . and made a circuit of the whole world in succession, leaving no part of the human race unvisited by the disease. Some cities were so severely afflicted as to be altogether depopulated, though in other places the visitation was less violent. . . . It seized upon some places at the commencement of winter, others in the course of the spring, others during the summer, and in some cases, when the autumn was advanced. . . . At the commencement of this calamity I was seized with what are termed buboes, while still a school boy, and lost by its recurrence at different times several of my children, my wife, and many of my kin, as well of my domestic and country servants.[8]

The most complete account of this plague appears in a work called *History of the Wars*, published in 550 by a man named Procopius. Procopius was an assistant to the general Belisarius and traveled with him throughout the empire during the time of Justinian's reconquest of the empire. He was in Constantinople in 542 and witnessed firsthand the plague there. "During these times," he writes, "there was a pestilence, by which the whole human race came near to being annihilated. Now in the case of all other scourges sent from heaven some explanation of a cause might be given by daring men . . . but for this calamity, it is quite impossible either to express in words or conceive in thought any explanation, except indeed to refer it to God."[9]

In his book Procopius describes the symptoms of the plague in great detail: "They had a sudden fever, some when just roused from sleep, others while walking about, and others while otherwise engaged, without any regard to what they were doing."[10] Procopius tells us that the fever was not severe at first, and that

> not one of those who contracted the disease expected to die from it. But on the same day in some cases, in others on the following day, and in the rest not many days later, a bubonic swelling developed; and this took place not only in the particular part of the body which is called the *boubon*, that is, "below the abdomen," [the groin] but also inside the armpit, and in some cases also beside the ears, and at different points on the thighs.[11]

Aside from these symptoms, which Procopius says were common to all victims, he describes other symptoms which varied from person to person:

> For there ensued with some a deep coma, with others a violent delirium. . . . Those who were under the spell of the coma forgot all those who were familiar to them and seemed to lie sleeping constantly. . . . But those who

were seized with delirium suffered from insomnia and a distorted imagination, and they would rush off in flight, crying out at the top of their voices. . . . And in those cases where neither coma nor delirium came on, the bubonic swelling became mortified [infected] and the sufferer, no longer able to endure the pain, died.[12]

The Spark That Starts a Pandemic

The plague had existed in African rats for centuries, so what caused it to suddenly explode as a human infection in the sixth century? Several factors combined at that particular time to make conditions ripe for a pandemic.

First, the flea that carries the plague bacterium *Xenopsylla cheopis* is most active within a very narrow temperature range—from about 59 degrees Fahrenheit (15 degrees Celsius) to about 68 degrees Fahrenheit (20 degrees Celsius). Also, at temperatures above 75 degrees Fahrenheit (23.9 degrees Celsius), the rate at which *Yersinia* builds up inside the flea slows down. If human plague made its first appearance in Egypt, which normally has a very warm climate, then something must have caused a significant drop in temperatures there in the mid-sixth century to bring the climate into the range favored by both the flea and the bacterium.

Using information gathered from studying tree rings, Irish scientist Mike Baillie showed that in fact such a drop in temperatures did occur in the mid- to late 530s. Scientists are not entirely sure what caused such a drop, but most theorize that it was caused by a dust veil—a large number of light-blocking particles in the atmosphere. The dust veil may have been caused by a comet shower, or it could have been caused by a volcanic eruption. Whatever the cause of the dust veil, it altered the North African climate enough for the plague to make its way to the coast and on to the rest of the ancient world.

Death came very quickly. As John of Ephesus wrote, "Nobody would go out of doors without a tag upon which his name was written and which hung on his neck or arm,"[13] so that he could be identified if he died suddenly.

The Origins of the Pandemic

Procopius and the others could not have known what actually caused plague or how it was spread, but in the port cities of the sixth century, the Mediterranean black rat was everywhere, living on and in the grain, cloth, spices, and other trade items brought there aboard ships from Africa, India, and the Orient. The rats tended to stay near the coast, where the food was, and food for a rat could be almost anything—even candles, soap, and paper. Their favorite food, however, was grain, so wherever people sent their grain, so went the rats. In the ancient Mediterranean world, grain was almost as valuable as gold, and whole fleets of ships carried grains (and rats) from Egypt to Rome, Constantinople, and throughout Europe. When the grain was transferred from ships to carts for transport to towns all over the empire, the rats were happy to stow away and feast on the cargo, so there was an abundance of healthy rats for plague-infected fleas to feed on.

Even writers who lived at the time disagree on the exact origin of Justinian's plague. Evagrius writes that it began in an area called Axum—the present-day African countries of Ethiopia and eastern Sudan. According to Procopius's account, it began in the port city of Pelusium, on the coast of Egypt at the eastern side of the Nile Delta. From there it spread west to Alexandria, one of the most important and populous port cities of the ancient world.

Out of Africa

At the end of 541, plague arrived in the eastern Mediterranean coast city of Gaza, then continued north to the cities of Ashkelon, Ashdod, and Rehovot, all coastal towns. In 542 it appeared in the holy city of Jerusalem and then in Antioch, a city as important as Constantinople and Alexandria. One of Antioch's holy men, Simeon Stylites, wrote, "In the whole region and in the city of Antioch, people were smitten with disease in the groin and armpits and were dying."[14]

The plague arrived in Constantinople that same year, starting, as always, on the docks. From there the rats carried their deadly cargo into the city. Like Rome, Constantinople was built on seven hills. Those living at the bottom of the hills fell ill first; those living higher up could see that it was coming, but could do nothing to stop it. Within a few weeks, the hospitals were overwhelmed, and the city's physicians could do nothing but try to keep the victims as comfortable as possible until they recovered or died. One of the few who survived was Justinian himself. During his illness he came close to death several times, and rumors of his death were common.

A Grave Situation

Once recovered, one of Justinian's major problems was how to handle the increasing numbers of the dead. The existing burial grounds filled very quickly, so large new ones were created and also filled. Cremation was prohibited to Christians at that

The plague arrived in Constantinople in A.D. 542, starting first at the docks of the city and then making its way to the highlands of the region.

time, so Justinian assigned an official named Theodorus to think of a solution, which he did. The new cemeteries that had been built were surrounded by protective walls that included 60-foot (18m) towers spaced evenly around them. Procopius describes Theodorus's unusual solution:

> And when it came about that all the tombs which had existed previously were filled with the dead, then they dug up all the places about the city one after the other, laid the dead there each one as he could, and departed; but later on those who were making these trenches, no longer able to keep up with the number of the dying, mounted the towers of the fortifications . . . and tearing off the roofs threw the bodies there in complete disorder . . . and filled practically all the towers with corpses, and then covered them again with their roofs. As a result, an evil stench pervaded the city and distressed the inhabitants still more, especially when the wind blew fresh from that quarter.[15]

The first wave of the disease lasted about four months, until so many rats and people had died that there was nowhere left for the bacteria to go. In his book *Justinian's Flea*, plague historian William Rosen writes:

> For one hundred days, Constantinople was a window onto Hell. Every day, one, two, sometimes five thousand of the city's residents . . . would become infected. A day's moderate fever would be followed by a week of delirium. Buboes would appear under the arms, in the groin, behind the ears, and grow to the size of melons. . . . Sometimes the buboes would burst in a shower of foul-smelling pus. Sometimes the plague would become . . . septicemic; those victims would die vomiting blood from internal hemorrhages that formed even more rapidly than the buboes. Those who contracted septicemic plague might have been the fortunate ones; though they all died, they at least died fast.[16]

That fall, plague made its appearance in the neighboring Persian empire—present-day Iraq, Iran, and parts of Pakistan and Afghanistan. By 545 widespread "famine, plague, madness, and fury"[17] gripped the land for two years. Once inside the Persian borders, the plague spread rapidly eastward, following Persian trade routes (including three more outbreaks in the unfortunate city of Antioch).

The Plague Goes West

The infection also spread to the west. A year after the plague took its horrible toll on Constantinople, it made its first appearance in the former Roman province of Gaul, modern-day France. In *The History of the Franks*, Roman historian and bishop Gregory of Tours writes,

When the plague finally began to rage, so many people were killed off throughout the whole region and the dead bodies were so numerous that it was not even possible

Roman historian and bishop Gregory of Tours wrote vividly about the effects of the plague in Gaul, modern-day France.

GRÉGOIRE DE TOURS

to count them. There was such a shortage of coffins and tombstones that ten or more bodies were buried in the same grave. In Saint Peter's church alone on a single Sunday three hundred dead bodies were counted. Death came very quickly. An open sore like a snake's bite appeared in the groin or the armpit, and the man who had it soon died of its poison, breathing his last on the second or third day.[18]

All throughout the sixth and seventh centuries, plague struck the ancient world again and again, subsiding in one locale only to flare up in another. It returned again to Constantinople in February 558, a disastrous year that had begun with a devastating earthquake that destroyed most of the Hagia Sophia. At least six more major outbreaks happened after 627. The one that occurred in 688–689, called the Plague of al-Jarif, is said to have killed two hundred thousand people in three days. Even though that number is likely to be exaggerated, it still suggests an enormous loss of life.

The Lasting Effects of Justinian's Plague

The Plague of Justinian killed at least 25 million people worldwide, wiped whole towns out of existence, and decimated the population of the empire for decades to come. It has been said by some historians that the Plague of Justinian was at least partially responsible for the final end of the Roman Empire and the rise of Europe and its individual nations.

Until the plague came, the population of the Byzantine Empire had been growing. After it struck, most of the towns and cities shrank in size or even disappeared entirely. In the first two years of the plague, about 4 million of the 26 million inhabitants of Justinian's empire had died. By the end of the sixth century the Byzantine population was down to only about 17 million. With so many adults dying, birthrates also declined, and this also contributed to the overall decline in population.

One of the most significant effects of this sharp decline in population was felt in the western part of the empire, in the

Western parts of the Byzantine empire recovered slowly from the effects of the plague, since the deaths of many farmers led to a decline in agriculture.

regions of Gaul and the rest of what would become western Europe, because of what it did to agriculture. The number of farmers left to work the land was significantly decreased. Those who owned the land were forced to pay more to the farmers who were left or else face the possibility that they would leave the land in search of a better life in towns and cities. As the farmers became more prosperous, their population began to rebound.

Another effect of the decreased population of farmers was that new labor-saving devices were introduced into western Europe. The plow, which was already being used in China and around the Mediterranean, was adapted to turn over the harder soils of Gaul and Germany. Since plows are more easily pulled by horses, the farmers needed to plant fields of oats to feed their horses, so they developed a three-field crop rotation system, replacing the two-field system they had before. Forests were cleared to create more arable (plantable) land. As the farmers became more productive, the western

European population recovered quickly—much more quickly than the populations in the eastern parts of the empire, where agriculture was not as important a part of the economy.

In the seventh century a new religion, Islam, arose in the Arabian Peninsula. With the rise of Europe and the weakening of Persia and Constantinople, largely because of the plague, Islam quickly became a powerful political force, filling in the power vacuum left by the Persians and the Byzantines and eventually conquering almost all of their lands. The histories of Europe and the Middle East were certainly shaped by the tiny *Yersinia pestis*.

The Black Death

The early fourteenth century was not a good time for the Chinese. In 1325, after having been conquered by the Mongolian empire under Genghis Khan, the country was ravaged by drought and a series of earthquakes. This was followed by a period of severe flooding and widespread famine that killed almost 8 million people. Then, in 1334 a mysterious and very deadly disease struck northeastern China. It was plague, but it was not the same as the Plague of Justinian. Carried not by rats but by large rodents called marmots, this kind of plague was especially malicious and explosive in its spread, with a special tendency to attack its victims' lungs. The marmot plague of central Asia spread rapidly and killed about 5 million people— about 90 percent of the population.

From China, the disease headed west and south, carried by Mongol conquerors and following military and trade routes, striking India, Syria, and Mesopotamia. In 1346 plague arrived at the Caspian Sea, attacking several towns, including Sarai, a busy slave market in the Mongol empire. The next year Mongol invaders brought the plague to Caffa (today called Feodosiya), a trading city just across the Black Sea from Constantinople. The invasion failed, as the Mongol army was all but destroyed by the disease they had brought. It is said that before giving up, the Mongol invaders launched their last attack on Caffa by using catapults to hurl the bodies of warriors who had died from plague over the walls of the city in order to spread the disease to the people inside. Whether the story is true or not,

A young boy is pictured with marmots killed by his father. Marmots were known to be carriers of bubonic plague in fourteenth-century Mongolia.

no accounts of life in Caffa by the end of that year exist, as the panic-stricken residents fled west across the Black Sea.

Late in 1347 Constantinople was once again devastated by the disease that had almost destroyed it eight hundred years earlier. A vivid description is written by Emperor John Cantacuzene, whose son died from the disease:

> [Some] had a very violent fever at first, the disease in such cases attacking the head; they suffered from speechlessness and insensibility to all happenings and then appeared as if sunken into a deep sleep. . . . Sputum suffused with blood was brought up and disgusting and stinking breath from within. . . . Great abscesses were formed on the legs or the arms, from which, when cut, a large quantity of foul-smelling pus flowed.[19]

Plague Comes to Europe

The trading town of Caffa had been founded by the Genoese, seafaring people from the Italian city of Genoa. When the plague struck, the Genoese in Caffa boarded their ships and fled across the Black Sea and the Mediterranean, back to Italy. By the time they got to Messina, on the island of Sicily (a journey of about three months), most of them were already dead. The survivors—those who had escaped infection and those who had survived the illness—were ordered to leave, but it was too late. "In their bones," writes Michael of Piazza, a Franciscan friar, "they bore so virulent a disease that anyone who only spoke to them was seized by a mortal illness and in no manner could evade death."[20] The great pestilence had arrived in Europe.

From Sicily the plague continued to spread rapidly from city to city—Genoa, Venice, Pisa, Florence, and Rome—and on throughout Italy. Everywhere, people died by the thousands, and the bodies piled up in the streets. One man from Siena writes:

> The mortality . . . began in May. It was a horrible thing, and I do not know where to begin to tell of the cruelty. Members of a household brought their dead to a ditch as best they could . . . as soon as those ditches were filled, more were dug. I, Agnolo diTura, buried my five children with my own hands. . . . And people said and believed, "This is the end of the world."[21]

From Italy the "mortality" traveled along the Mediterranean coast west to France. It struck Avignon, where Pope Clement VI was living at the time. It crossed over the Pyrenees in southern France and spread throughout Spain. It continued north through Europe, ravaging Germany, and invaded the Scandinavian countries even as far north as Iceland and Greenland. In 1348 it arrived in England and Ireland.

The Plague in England

The early fourteenth century was also not a good time to be English. After two centuries of warm summers, mild winters,

Giovanni Boccaccio and the *Decameron*

Giovanni Boccaccio was an Italian poet and a resident of Flor-ence, Italy, when the plague struck his town in 1348. He survived and later wrote a book, now considered a classic of Renaissance literature, called the *Decameron*. The *Decameron* is a collection of stories set in a country home, where a group of ten wealthy young people has gathered to escape the plague in Florence. There they pass the time eating, drinking, and telling stories. Since Boccaccio was an eyewitness, the *Decameron* is a valuable description of the experience of the plague in Florence, espe-cially in its prologue, in which he writes:

> Into the distinguished city of Florence . . . there came the deadly pestilence . . . and it killed an infinite number of people. . . . It began in both men and women with certain swellings either in the groin or under the armpits, some of which grew to the size of a normal apple and others to the size of an egg. . . . Let me say, then, that the power of the plague described here was of such virulence in spreading from one person to another that not only did it spread from one man to the next, but what's more, it was often transmitted from the garments of a sick or dead man to animals. . . . Oh, how many great palaces, beautiful homes, and noble dwellings . . . were now emptied, down to the last servant! How many valiant men, beautiful women, and charming young men, who might have been pronounced very healthy by Galen, Hippocrates, and Aesculapius, dined in the morning with their relatives, and then in the evening took supper with their ancestors in the other world!

Quoted in Wendy Orent, *Plague: The Mysterious Past and Terrifying Future of the World's Most Deadly Disease.* New York: Free Press, 2004, pp. 119–20.

plenty of rainfall, and good harvests, the summers of 1316 and 1317 were disastrous. The temperature dropped, the summers shortened, it rained too much, the crops failed, and famine was widespread. Those who survived starvation were left undernourished and ill-equipped to resist the pestilence that arrived in 1348.

Historians believe that this especially vicious kind of plague may have spread as rapidly as 2 to 4 miles (3.2 to 6.4km) a day. Everywhere it went, the story was the same—whole towns were wiped out, those who dared care for the sick were soon stricken as well, and the numbers of dead soon overwhelmed the ability of the living to bury them. The plague caused such terror in people that family members abandoned their sick relatives and left

Guy de Chauliac, physician to Pope Clement VI, wrote that many doctors deserted the sick for fear of being infected themselves.

Plague and the Peasants' Revolt

After the Black Death, as the rich saw their wealth disappear and poor laborers and peasant farmers become wealthier, they took measures to stop the trend. In 1349 and 1351, King Edward III of England made it illegal for workers to demand wages higher than they had been before the plague. It also became illegal for workers to refuse work or to leave their villages to look for better wages somewhere else. In the 1370s a series of new taxes, called poll taxes, were placed on laborers. These measures led to a great deal of resentment between the classes. Finally, in 1381 the tension exploded in what came to be called the Peasants' Revolt.

In June of that year, sixty thousand angry men from the towns of Kent and Essex marched in London to protest the new laws and taxes. On June 14 the rebels met with the new king, Richard II, who was only fourteen years old at the time. The king told them their demands would be met. But that same day, a group of rebels invaded the Tower of London and killed several royal officials, including the Archbishop of Canterbury, the most important church official in England. At another meeting the next day, the king agreed to more of the rebels' demands, but during the meeting the mayor of London pulled one of the rebel leaders from his horse and killed him. He then raised a force of about seven thousand men and effectively crushed the rebellion. The main rebel leaders were executed, and most of the king's promises were not kept. Although the Peasants' Revolt was considered a failure, after it happened landowners treated the peasants with more respect, and the poll taxes were abolished for good.

them to fend for themselves. According to a manuscript from a French abbey, "A father did not dare to go and visit his son, nor a brother his sister, and people could not be found to nurse one another, because, when the person breathed the breath of another he could not escape."[22]

People deserted the cities by the thousands. Law and order collapsed. Public services ceased to exist, and doctors brave enough to stay and tend to the sick were helpless to do much of anything. Their helplessness is illustrated by Guy de Chauliac, the physician to Pope Clement VI: "It was useless and shameful for the doctors, the more so as they dared not visit the sick, for fear of being infected. And when they did visit them, they did hardly anything for them, and were paid nothing; for all the sick died, except some few at the last who escaped, the buboes being ripened."[23]

Treating Plague in the Fourteenth Century

Terrified and desperate, people looked for answers from their doctors and other medical practitioners such as local "wise women." By this time a great deal of new medical knowledge had been contributed by Islamic physicians and philosophers. They studied their patients very closely and learned much about the nature of illnesses and fevers. They were especially skilled at treating eye diseases. This was also the time of the rise of great universities and schools of medicine in Europe and the Middle East, and university-trained physicians were considered far superior to all other health practitioners. The number of hospitals for care of the sick, the elderly, and the mentally ill also grew during this time. Despite these advancements, however, medical thought in Europe had changed very little since the time of Justinian's Plague. It was still based largely on philosophical and religious explanations instead of scientific ones. The major principle in medical thought was still the idea of the balance of the "humors," or main fluids of the body.

A Foul Stench

Since the humoral theory could not come close to explaining the catastrophe in terms of simple fluid imbalance, many physicians of the time were convinced that the plague was actually an airborne disease, caused by the foul stench of decaying flesh, or "miasma," that floated in the air around infected people. (They had no idea how close they actually were to the truth.) Because of this, many people, especially the wealthy, fled the towns to the country to try to avoid the evil air. Some who could not or would not flee tried using scents to ward off the smell. They carried flowers or sweet-smelling herbs, or burned incense, or held cloths dipped in aromatic oil to their faces. They kept their doors and windows tightly closed and hung thick cloths over them to keep out the deadly air. Doctors told people not to sleep on their backs, because this would make it easier for miasmas to get into their lungs. The pope in Avignon, France, sat between two large fires, believing that this would cleanse his air of poisonous miasmas.

Terrified people were willing to try anything to keep from getting sick. The more superstitious among them bought all kinds of charms and spells to protect themselves. Some believed that sound could drive the disease away; they rang church bells or fired cannons. With the exception of the hands and feet, bathing was considered to be dangerous because it opened one's pores and made it easier for the disease to get into the body. For four hundred years, until the plague finally disappeared from Europe, Europeans refrained from regular bathing.

The medieval doctors could do very little to treat their patients suffering with plague. Herbs, potions, and salves were offered to try to calm the patients and ease their pain. Bloodletting with leeches or scalpels was done to try to restore humoral balance, but not only did it not help the patients, it often hastened death from blood loss. Buboes were sometimes lanced with a knife to drain the pus inside, and while this helped relieve some of the pain they caused, it did nothing to stop the disease. A strong person could possibly survive the bubonic form but had no hope of surviving pneumonic plague; the person who began to spit blood was considered terminal.

Religion and the Plague

As Christianity grew and became more influential, the Church taught that illness was divine punishment for sin, sent by God, and that the only way to recover was to repent of one's sins or make a pilgrimage to a holy place. The Church still frowned

The Flagellants

One of the more bizarre reactions to the plague appeared in Germany—a strange and mysterious brotherhood known as the Flagellants, or the Brethren of the Cross. The members of the brotherhood were among those who believed that the plague was brought on by the anger of God as punishment for sin. They believed that no amount of confession or changing one's ways was enough to satisfy God, so the Flagellants punished themselves. Groups of two or three hundred men, sometimes with women included, would march along the roads in long columns, two by two, keeping their eyes fixed downward toward the ground, moving from town to town. They wore black robes with red crosses and hid their faces with large hoods. When they reached a town, they would announce their presence, and a crowd would gather. They would then form a large circle, throw off their robes, and fall to the ground. The leaders would then go around the circle and beat them with whips or clubs. After a while, the entire group would get up and each man would beat his own back with a scourge, a stick with three ropes attached that each ended in a knot studded with tiny iron spikes. They hoped that their cries of pain would reach heaven and appease God's anger. Some even died during the ritual punishment. This went on all over Germany and parts of France until Pope Clement VI finally ordered it stopped. Ironically, rather than help stop the spread of the plague, the Flagellants are thought to have spread it everywhere they went.

upon scientific experimentation, and dissection of human bodies was strictly prohibited, which contributed to the slow progress of medical knowledge in Europe. Many people did not consider medicine a proper occupation for a Christian because it was seen as interfering with God's will. Traditional folk medicine, with its emphasis on spells, magic, and herbal treatments, was condemned and had to either change in order to fit in with Christian teaching or else be practiced in secret.

Other Explanations

Many people felt that the cause of the plague was neither medical nor religious. The idea of balance of the humors failed to explain it because so many people were falling ill and dying so quickly, and because no treatment was doing any good at all. The Church also was unable to provide a satisfactory answer, because all kinds of people were dying, both good and bad, and no amount of prayer or pilgrimage did any good.

Having lost faith in their priests and their doctors, people looked for someone or something else to blame. Astrology was one culprit; a group of professors from the University of Paris declared that the plague was caused by the unfortunate place of the feared planet Saturn in the house of Jupiter. Many people decided that the pestilence was the work of wicked people. Often, those who lived outside mainstream society—the beggars, the crippled, or the insane—were made scapegoats, accused of witchcraft, and stoned, beaten, or burned to death.

Desperate for an explanation, a group of professors declared that the plague was caused by the unfortunate place of the feared planet Saturn (pictured) in the house of Jupiter.

Many in predominantly Christian Europe decided to blame the Jews for the catastrophe. The Jews of Europe had been persecuted for centuries, and now a period of especially violent anti-Semitism, or hatred toward Jews, began. It made no difference that Jews were dying as quickly as Christians. In Germany, eleven Jews were accused of deliberately poisoning the wells, from which Christians drew their water, with the plague. They were put on trial and tortured until they "confessed." The false confessions did not save them, however; they were condemned to death, dragged out of their homes and burned in the streets. Two hundred Jews were killed in Basel, Switzerland, and another two thousand in Strassbourg, Germany. Despite efforts by Pope Clement to stop the killing, these scenes were repeated all over Europe.

The Effects of the Black Death

By the early 1350s the worst of the Black Death finally was past, leaving a permanent stamp on the nature of European society. Historians sometimes think of European history in two parts—before the Black Death and after it—because every aspect of medieval life was forever changed by it. Medieval economy, religion, and medical practice were especially changed by this epic disaster.

Economic Upheaval

The European economic structure was probably the most affected by the Black Death and its catastrophic population decline. In the towns, so many skilled craftsmen were lost that valuable skills such as blacksmithing, shoe making, and wood carving were almost lost as well. As a result of the shortage of workers, the cost of their labor and everything they made rose sharply.

The deserted and neglected countryside was no better off. In his book *The Great Mortality*, historian John Kelly writes of "hulking pockets of survivors surrounded by untended fields, unmended fences, unrepaired bridges, abandoned farms, overgrown orchards, half-empty villages, and crumbling buildings,

Homes, buildings, and barns, like this fourteenth-century barn in England, were largely abandoned by those fleeing from the plague.

and hovering over everything was the oppressive sound of silence."[24]

Higher prices for goods and a much lower supply of workers meant that traditional roles for the rich and the poor were reversed. Wealthy landholders began to see their wealth disappear as the cost of goods and services skyrocketed. At the same time, because so few people were left to feed, demand for food grown in their fields decreased, and agricultural prices fell. Many landholders, who depended on the production of their lands for their income, could no longer afford to keep their land and simply abandoned it.

On the other hand, as had happened after Justinian's Plague, workers who survived soon realized that they could demand higher wages from those who hired them because there were so few of them left. Serfs, or peasant farmers, who had lived on and farmed the lands of the wealthy, were no longer tied to the estates of their lords, because they knew they could be hired anywhere they went. Also, with so much abandoned farmland available, they could choose not to work for anyone else at all and settle wherever they chose. Peasants became wealthier; the wealthy became poorer and less powerful.

The Church and Religion After the Plague

For centuries the Church had held enormous power and influence over the daily lives of the European people. After the Black Death, the Church found much of its authority eroded, for several reasons. First, many people had lost faith in the Church when their priests were unable to do anything to help them. Hundreds of them had fled the towns in fear of the plague, and the people became disillusioned and angry with their clergy for abandoning their Christian duties. Also, the plague had caused a critical shortage of clerics—priests, monks, nuns, and other religious people—because so many of them had perished. To make up for the shortage, poorly trained boys and men who were not suited to the religious life were allowed to become priests.

After the plague, many people began to practice their faith in private family chapels rather than in established churches, and they began to develop their own methods and traditions of worship that were different from those of the established Church. Some historians believe that the Black Death and the Church's failures during it were a factor in the eventual rise of Protestant churches in the sixteenth century.

Innovations in Medicine

Like the Church, the medical profession also came out of the plague years with its reputation damaged. Not even the most highly trained physicians had been able to do anything to stop the disease or help those who suffered from it. After the plague, medical thought drifted away from traditional Greek and Roman philosophical approaches to medicine and focused more on practical observation of diseases. The influence of university-trained physicians, so highly regarded before, diminished in favor of those who learned their skills through hands-on practice, and surgeons found new respect among their patients. Medical textbooks were published in languages other than Latin, which only the university doctors could read. Despite the objections of the Church, autopsies, which had been illegal for centuries, became more common, and a great deal was learned about the inner workings of the human body. Physicians began actually to test their theories about illness, with real patients, to learn whether they were accurate. This marked the beginning of the modern scientific method. Doctors also began to learn more about how diseases spread, and new ideas about public health and hygiene appeared.

The hospital system also changed because of the plague. During the Black Death, some of the larger cities built pest-

After the plague, autopsies—which had been illegal for centuries— became more common, and a great deal was learned about the inner workings of the human body.

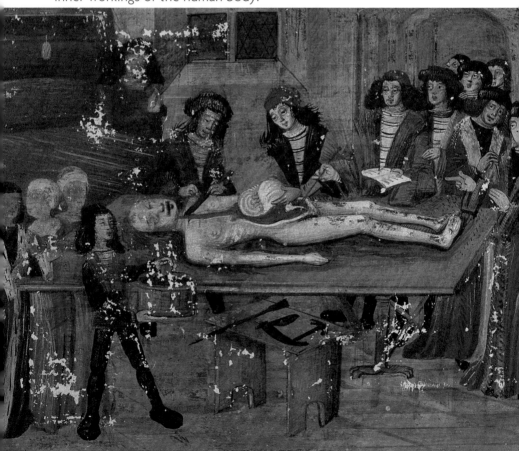

houses, specifically for plague victims, but the great majority of the patients who went there were the poor, as conditions there were abysmal. Some English pesthouses were nothing more than a group of small huts that could handle only a few patients at a time. Most people saw them as places where the poor went to die, after which their bodies would be thrown into mass graves called plague pits. Old hospitals that had been used for housing leprosy patients were now used for plague victims, since leprosy—the most feared disease until the Black Death—had declined sharply.

After the Black Death, hospitals started to look more like their modern form. Instead of just housing dying people, hospitals now at least tried to cure illness and help the patient to recover. Also at this time, wards developed, in which patients with similar illnesses were grouped together, and health workers became more skilled at taking care of them.

Out of the Dark Ages

Before that first plague ship sailed into the harbor at Messina, Europe had been locked into a pattern of poverty, hunger, oppression, and technological stagnation. Wealthy lords ruled over impoverished peasants with an iron fist. New ideas and inventions were considered dangerous or heretical, and the Church strictly controlled every aspect of life. This was the period of time known as the Dark Ages. Despite the horrific suffering that the Black Death inflicted on Europe, it led to such massive changes in medieval society that the deadlock was broken, and Europe embarked on a new period of invention, ideas, and prosperity—the period known as the Renaissance.

The Plague Returns to London

The Black Death was not the last time Europeans would see the plague. Over the next three hundred years, it would come back, again and again. These repeated outbreaks kept the population of Europe below pre-plague levels for two centuries.

Because of the active sea trading activity between English ports and the rest of Europe, England saw the plague return at least sixteen times in the sixteenth and seventeenth centuries. London, because it was a major port city and because of its high populations of both humans and rats, was especially hard hit by these outbreaks. None of them, though, came even close in numbers of deaths to the Great Plague that hit London in 1665.

At the beginning of that year, about five hundred thousand people lived in London, many of them in poverty. Their muddy streets and open sewers were filled with trash, garbage, and human waste. Rats and other vermin flourished. It was the perfect setting for a major plague outbreak.

Almost half of London's citizens fled the city immediately, including all the members of Parliament, the entire royal court, and those in the merchant classes. Many people, however, did not have the financial resources to leave the city, and London officials took steps to keep them from leaving and spreading the disease. Any family that had even one ill member could not leave their home for forty days. Their doors and windows were nailed shut, a watchman was posted outside, and a red cross was painted on their door to warn others not to go in. This basically amounted to a death sentence for the whole family. London resident Samuel Pepys, who became famous for his extensive diary, writes on June 7, 1665, "This day I did in Drury Lane see two or three houses marked with a red cross upon their doors and 'Lord have mercy upon us' writ there, which was a sad sight to me, being the first of the kind that . . . I ever saw."[25]

At its peak late that summer, the Great Plague of 1665 was killing almost four thousand Londoners every week. It may have been more—Jews and Quakers were not counted. By October the outbreak finally subsided but did not completely disappear until the following September, when the famous Great Fire of London destroyed most of the city, along with most of its rats. Of the three hundred thousand people who had stayed in London, the plague took as many as ninety-seven thousand

Casualties this Week.

Impofthume	11
Infants	16
Killed by a fall from the Belfrey at Alhallows the Great	1
Kingfevil	2
Lethargy	1
Palfie	1
Plague	7165
Rickets	17

The plague returned to England several times. In one week over seven thousand people died from the plague, as shown in this 1665 London death register.

lives, most of them poor. In 1669 only two plague deaths were recorded, and other diseases became of greater concern. "The smallpox [is] very much in London,"[26] writes London citizen Thomas Rugge in his diary in 1668. The Great Plague of 1665 was the last wave of plague to strike England. By 1680 plague had disappeared from England, although public health authorities kept the column for plague deaths in their record books until 1703.

CHAPTER FOUR

The Third Pandemic

By the mid-1700s plague had all but disappeared from the European continent. Outbreaks were confined mostly to northern Africa and much of Asia, areas where plague had always existed. In the late 1700s a new strain of plague, called Orientalis, appeared in Yunnan Province in south-western China. It was carried by rats but was deadly to people as well. In 1792 a young poet from Yunnan named Shi Tao-nan wrote:

> Dead rats in the east, dead rats in the west!
> As if they were tigers, indeed the people are scared.
> A few days following the death of the rats, men pass away
>   like falling walls!
> The coming of the devil of plague suddenly makes the
>   lamp dim,
> Then it is blown out, leaving man, ghost, and corpse in the
>   dark room.[27]

Shi Tao-nan died of the plague a few days after this poem was written.

From Yunnan in the southwest the plague spread eastward along trade routes to Pakhoi, a port city almost a thousand miles away. Major outbreaks occurred there in 1877 and again in 1882. From there it quickly reached the major ports of Canton and Hong Kong, and then traveled across the Pacific on ships bound for the Americas.

At about the same time that the Orientalis rat plague was making its way into North America, a different and far deadlier strain of plague was terrorizing a part of northeastern China called Manchuria. This was marmot plague, different from the rat-borne Orientalis variety, but very similar to the kind that had ravaged Europe during the Black Death. In three separate waves—in 1910, 1917, and 1920—this highly virulent kind of plague killed almost a hundred thousand people. The third pandemic, then, was really two separate pandemics—rat plague and marmot plague—occurring at about the same time.

An Explosion of Knowledge

Between the time of the 1665 Great Plague of London and this new plague pandemic, important discoveries about the nature of microbes and how they cause disease had burst onto the scene. In 1675, just ten years after the Great Plague, Dutch scientist Antoni van Leeuwenhoek had become the first actually to see bacteria with the microscope that he had designed.

In the late 1700s the plague reached the major ports of Canton and Hong Kong, eventually spreading to the Americas in the late 1800s.

Then, in the early 1800s a new infectious disease appeared in the world. Asian cholera, which had started in India and spread into Russia, killed thousands and brought the same kind of terror that the plague had caused centuries earlier. In response to this new threat, European physicians and scientists came together in a series of three major conferences, starting in Paris in 1851. At these conferences they shared their knowledge with each other, hoping to come up with an effective way to contain the spread of cholera as well as other infectious diseases.

A major breakthrough occurred in 1850, when scientists discovered the organism that causes the disease anthrax in cattle and showed how the illness could be transmitted to healthy

French scientist Louis Pasteur published his groundbreaking work on several infectious diseases in the mid-1800s, but the cause of the plague remained a mystery.

animals by injecting them with the organism. Later that same decade, French scientist Louis Pasteur published his ground-breaking work on the cause, treatment, and transmission of several infectious diseases, including anthrax and rabies. German scientist Robert Koch added to the growing body of knowledge by improving techniques for staining organisms so they could be better seen and identified under the microscope. By the 1890s the organisms for many diseases, such as leprosy, malaria, tetanus, tuberculosis, and pneumonia, had been identified. Plague, however, remained a mystery.

The Asian pandemic provided the opportunity to solve the mystery. What it taught about plague provided doctors with new weapons to combat all kinds of infectious diseases. It also opened a window on both Justinian's Plague and the Black Death, offering historians new insight into those earlier pandemics. The story of the third pandemic is the story of the scientists who opened that window.

The Plague Arrives at the Coast

In the spring of 1894, the Orientalis plague arrived in Canton (today called Guangzhou), a city of a million and a half people in southern China. Canton had important trading relationships with Europe and the Americas, and people feared that another worldwide pandemic might occur. Doctors and scientists from many countries descended on China in an effort to study the disease firsthand. One of the first on the scene in Canton was James Lowson, director of medical services in the British colony of Hong Kong, a small peninsula on the southeastern coast of China. He had heard that the plague was spreading to Hong Kong, and by May 10 twenty cases had been reported in the hospital there.

Lowson left Canton and returned to Hong Kong, where he turned the ship *Hygea* into a floating hospital. Soon he was overwhelmed with cases of plague. On May 13, he writes in his diary, "Hot sun. Cases pouring in. Outlook appalling."[28] Twenty-five people died that day, and twelve more ill people arrived at the ship. The next day, twenty-two more died. Lowson knew he could not handle the crisis himself and sent out a plea for help to other doctors who might know more about how to manage the disease. Seven weeks later, two experts in microbiology, one Japanese and one French, arrived in Hong Kong. The race to identify the plague organism quickly became a competition between the two scientists—Shibasaburo Kitasato and Alexandre Yersin.

The Race Is On

Kitasato arrived first, and with a whole team of assistants and lots of publicity. The British colonial government provided him with everything he needed—money, a modern hospital with up-to-date medical equipment, and plenty of patients (both dead and alive) for him to use to study the disease. Yersin arrived three days later, alone (an assistant had run off with all his money). He had to settle for a small hut in which to work. He had no equipment except a microscope and an autoclave, a machine for sterilizing objects. To get bodies to study he had to bribe British soldiers assigned to dispose of the dead. He was not even permitted to enter the hospital. It looked as if Kitasato had the advantage in this "competition." Then, one of Kitasato's assistants made a serious mistake. He had performed an autopsy on a dead patient without using any kind of bed or protective mosquito netting. He kept the deceased patients in a large warehouse where disease-carrying mosquitoes could freely enter at night. Kitasato discovered that the blood of his patients contained two different types of bacteria, one of which was associated with pneumonia. With his samples contaminated by another kind of bacteria, the cause of death of the patients could not be confirmed, and the plague organism could not be positively identified.

On the other side, Yersin, in his small hut with only minimal equipment, was able to isolate large amounts of bacilli (rod-shaped bacteria) from the blood of his test subjects. In his journal he writes, "At first glance, I see a real mass of bacilli, all identical. They are very small rods, thick with rounded ends and lightly colored."[29] He brought his samples back to Paris to

Alexandre Yersin

Alexandre Yersin was a French scientist and doctor who is known for his work with many diseases but is best known as the discoverer of the bacterium that causes plague.

Yersin was born in Switzerland in 1863, the son of a science teacher. As a child, Yersin was very interested in nature. He decided to study medicine and was educated in Switzerland, Germany, and Paris, France, where he joined Louis Pasteur's research laboratory. While there, he worked with bacteriologist Émile Roux to help discover the toxin made by the diphtheria organism, and he helped to perfect the rabies vaccine first developed by Roux and Pasteur.

In 1890 Yersin left Europe and signed on as a ship's doctor on board a steamer bound for Saigon, Vietnam, and Manila in the Philippines. Four years later he was sent by the French government to Hong Kong to research the epidemic of bubonic and pneumonic plague that was sweeping across China. Only seven days after he arrived, he isolated the plague bacterium and named it *Pasteurella pestis,* after Louis Pasteur. In addition, he discovered that the disease also lived in rodents, paving the way for the discovery of how plague is transmitted. Back in Paris, he developed an antiplague serum and then returned to Vietnam, where he established a laboratory at Nha Trang to produce the serum, using blood from horses, but it did not work very well. He spent the rest of his life working to improve the health care of the people of Southeast Asia. Yersin died in 1943 and was buried at Nha Trang. In 1970 *Pasteurella pestis* was renamed *Yersinia pestis* in his honor.

French scientist Alexandre Yersin discovered the bacterium that causes plague.

be identified. Scientists there injected the samples into test animals, which then developed plague symptoms. Yersin's bacilli were confirmed as the organism of plague. Yersin named it *Pasteurella pestis*, in honor of Yersin's mentor, Louis Pasteur.

The Next Hurdle

The next step in the process was to discover the plague reservoir—where the bacteria live before they infect a person. Both Yersin and Kitasato had noticed large numbers of dead rats in Hong Kong. Yersin quickly discovered that the blood of the rats was teeming with plague bacteria. He also noted the connection between poor living conditions, rats, and plague. In a paper written in 1894, he writes:

> In the infected boroughs, many dead rats are found on the ground. . . . The lodging quarters of the poor Chinese are often so revoltingly dirty that one scarcely has the courage to enter them. In addition, the number of occupants is unbelievable. One can imagine the havoc that can be caused by an epidemic on such a terrain and the difficulty involved in its control.[30]

The question remained, however, of how the bacteria got from the rat to people. The role of the vector, or insect carrier, had not yet been discovered, although it was suspected. In 1897 a Japanese doctor named Masanori Ogata wrote, "One should pay attention to insects like fleas for, as the rat becomes cold after death, they leave their host and may transmit the plague directly to man."[31] Kitasato did not believe in the insect theory. He believed that the spread happened in one of three ways—through an open wound on the skin, by ingestion (eating rat meat), or by breathing it in. Yersin did not believe those theories. Instead, he thought an insect might be the transmitting factor. He tested his theory by grinding up dead fleas found in his laboratory and injecting the material into guinea pigs. Yersin writes, "The inoculum contained a large number of bacilli which were similar to the plague organism and the

Shibasaburo Kitasato (1853–1931) was one of two scientists brought to Hong Kong by the British colonial government to find the cause of the bubonic plague.

guinea pigs died in forty-eight hours with the specific lesions of the disease."[32] Yersin was unable, however, to demonstrate a definite connection between rat, flea, and human. That was left to another scientist—a Frenchman named Paul-Louis Simond.

The Connection Is Made

Simond had come to Bombay, India, in 1897 to help fight the plague epidemic that was raging there. Like Yersin, he was a member of the Pasteur Institute in Paris and had worked with many of the same scientists as Yersin. His original assignment there was to test the value of an antiplague serum developed at the institute. The results were not very successful, but Simond stayed on to continue Yersin's work. Like Yersin, Simond was not convinced of the generally accepted theories about how plague was transmitted. Researchers in India believed that rats got plague by eating the corpses of other rats that had already died from it. They also believed that humans picked it up through cuts on their feet. Simond showed that rats almost never got plague when they were fed infected food. He also pointed out that human plague victims did not always have cuts or cracks on their feet.

Simond discovered that pricking the feet of rats with infected needles almost always caused plague in the rats. He wondered if an insect that bit a human could transmit plague in that way. He examined his patients and found that some of them had small blisters, usually on their lower legs, which were full of plague bacteria. Patients with these blisters always developed buboes near the blister. He felt sure the blisters were caused by an insect bite, but he was not sure which insect it was. Knowing that rats carried plague, that they were often

The rat flea, whose guts are filled with *Y. pestis* bacilli, regurgitates infected blood when it bites, thus infecting the victim, or host.

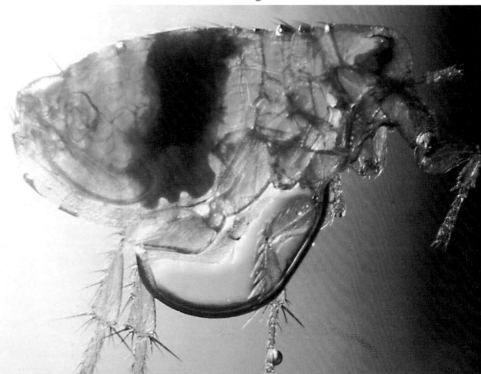

infested with fleas, and that fleas often bit people (which many people did not believe at that time), he made the connection between the three. He conducted several experiments, including one that showed that healthy rats could not get plague without the presence of fleas. He also examined rat fleas under the microscope and found their gut filled with plague bacilli.

Other researchers had trouble duplicating Simond's results, and few of them believed in his conclusions. British plague scientists considered his work "so weak as to be hardly deserving of consideration."[33] Other researchers wrote that "plague infected fleas are of no practical importance in regard to the spread of plague."[34] Meanwhile, the epidemic raged on, and ships sailing from the port carried the infection to the rest of the world, including North America.

Plague Comes to America

In 1899 a ship sailed from Hong Kong, bound for San Francisco, California. On board were eleven stowaways, two of whom were ill with plague. When the ship docked, the stowaways were discovered, and the ship was quarantined. Later, their bodies were found floating in San Francisco Bay. Autopsies showed that they both carried the plague bacterium. No other cases were found on the ship, but no one thought to watch for rats, which still lived on almost every cargo ship as they had for centuries. In March 1900, a city health official performed an autopsy on a deceased Chinese man and found organisms in his blood that looked like *Y. pestis*.

Quick action was needed in order to prevent an epidemic, but quick action did not come. Health officials in the city did not believe that rats or fleas had anything to do with plague. Instead, they decided to quarantine thousands of Asians, especially Chinese, who had come to California in the late 1800s. At the same time, California politicians, including the governor, refused to believe that plague was in their state, worried about what such news would do to the state's economy. By the time a new governor took office in 1903, no one could deny that plague was in San Francisco. By 1904, 127 people had gotten plague; all but 4 died from it. After that, cases dropped off. Then, in 1906 a huge earthquake hit San Francisco, leaving much of the city in ruins and thousands of people homeless. Plague cases surged again, along with the rat population. Finally, city officials accepted the idea of rats as plague carriers and began a massive rat roundup, offering money for every animal brought in. The effort succeeded in stopping the epidemic.

In 1908 the British Plague Commission, which ten years earlier had ridiculed Simond for his ideas, finally confirmed that plague was indeed transmitted to humans by rats and fleas. In their report, Simond was given no credit for his work.

The Marmot Plague of Manchuria

While authorities in San Francisco struggled with Orientalis plague, people back in China were struggling with a much more dangerous and virulent plague.

For centuries, the native peoples of Manchuria had held a traditional belief that tribal hunters, after death, would live their next life as a marmot, the large groundhog-like rodents that they hunted for their skins and for food. According to the tradition, however, one part of the marmot could never be eaten—the fatty area near the animal's armpits—because they believed that this was where the dead hunter's soul lived.

Like most ancient beliefs, this one had a grain of reason to it. The armpit, or axilla, is where a large cluster of lymph glands is located and where the plague bacillus collects in an infected host animal. Manchurian hunters knew well the dangers of handling a sick marmot, and if one was killed, it was given to the dogs.

In the mid-1800s hunters from Russia started moving into Manchuria to hunt marmots for their valuable skins, but they did not listen to the warnings of the Manchurians about sick animals. They were careless with the bodies of dead marmots, and accounts from the time tell of whole families dying of pneumonic plague, along with anyone who came in contact with them. By the turn of the century, marmot fur was in great demand in Western countries, and Manchuria had an abundant supply. Russian, Chinese, and Japanese immigrants poured into the area, also paying little attention to the native Manchurians. In the early 1900s, the small outbreaks exploded into full-scale epidemics with the coming of the new railroad through Manchuria. Pneumonic plague traveled with the immigrants and spread like wildfire in the overcrowded and filthy towns that sprang up along the rail lines.

Wu Lien-teh, Plague Fighter

Wu Lien-teh was born in 1879 in Penang, Malaysia, an island country in Southeast Asia. He was a gifted student in school and won a scholarship to study at Cambridge University in England. During his time at Cambridge, he was awarded several prizes for his scholarship. After graduation in 1902, he continued his studies in England, Germany, Paris, and Baltimore, Maryland. These experiences sparked an interest in Western medical ideas.

In 1907 he went to China to become director of the Imperial Medical College at Tientsin. Three years later he was appointed head of a medical team assigned to help fight the terrible plague epidemic that was raging in Manchuria. In 1912 he established the Manchurian Plague Prevention Service. Despite the fact that almost every one of his patients died, including half his medical team, Wu persevered. His insistence that everyone exposed to plague wear protective gauze masks helped contain the epidemic. Wu gained worldwide renown for his courageous work in Manchuria. He also helped modernize the Chinese health care system and Chinese medical education. He published a great deal of work on plague, cholera, anthrax, and other diseases. In 1959 he published his autobiography *Plague Fighter: The Autobiography of a Modern Chinese Physician.* Wu died in 1960 at the age of eighty-one.

Controlling the Marmot Plague

The local government in the area was unprepared to deal with the epidemic. They enlisted the help of a young Chinese doctor named Wu Lien-teh, who had been educated at Cambridge University in England. Wu had experience in bacteriology and was very interested in Western medical practices. He was immediately sent to the city of Harbin, a major stop along the railway, and very hard-hit by the plague. The doctors at the hospital there did not believe that the plague was contagious between people. They did not understand that marmot plague, unlike the rat-borne Orientalis variety, had a special tendency to head straight to the lungs. Despite Wu's warnings, they would not wear the gauze masks that he offered. That changed after several of the hospital's workers, including their plague expert, died of the disease. Wu became the head of the anti-plague effort, and doctors and workers from several countries joined him in Harbin. A massive quarantine effort was begun, and although no one who got sick survived, his efforts helped to prevent many more cases from starting.

During the Manchurian plague epidemic, nearly sixty thousand people died. Here, horses transport infected corpses to a location where hundreds of bodies were burned.

As in the first two pandemics, a major problem was the disposal of the dead. It was winter in Manchuria, and the ground was frozen solid. Many ill people had died in the streets and had frozen where they lay. Wu knew that plague can live in frozen tissue and that the bodies had to be burned. To do this, he had to get permission from the emperor of China, because cremation was forbidden. Hundreds of frozen bodies were burned in huge fires, and the ashes were buried in the earth, thawed by the fires. Gradually, Wu's efforts paid off, and the death rate finally subsided. By 1911 the Manchurian pneumonic plague had spread over a thousand miles and had killed sixty thousand people.

Plague Strikes Again

A second wave of pneumonic plague broke out in November 1917, this time in Inner Mongolia, a northern Chinese province that borders on Manchuria. Again, Wu reported to one of the hardest-hit areas, joining two American doctors who were already there. The spread of the disease was worsened by the Chinese government's refusal to allow Wu and his partners to work. Despite this obstacle, the outbreak subsided by the spring of 1918. About sixteen thousand people died.

A third major outbreak revisited Manchuria in 1920, but this time the Manchurian authorities were more knowledgeable and better prepared. Again, Wu and his team led the control efforts, which started right away. By the time the spread was stopped the following year, about ninety-three hundred people had died—relatively few compared to the earlier outbreaks.

Lessons Learned

Some very important lessons about pneumonic plague were learned because of the Manchurian and Mongolian epidemics of pneumonic plague. Although the connection between pneumonic plague in marmots and that in humans had been strongly suspected, it was the work of American plague expert Richard Pearson Strong that confirmed it. He demonstrated that healthy marmots could catch plague when the bacillus

Doctors discovered that pneumonic plague bacteria can travel about six feet when a person coughs or sneezes.

was sprayed at them in droplet form similar to a sneeze. Wu, Strong, and other scientists were able to show that marmots can get not only flea-borne bubonic plague but also that they are the only animal besides humans that can get and spread pneumonic plague to each other.

Later experiments showed that pneumonic plague can travel about 6 feet (1.8m) by coughing or sneezing but is rarely spread by talking. Doctors also learned that pneumonic plague can live on floors and in clothing and bedding and that it can live up to eight hours in direct sunlight—something bubonic plague cannot do.

Although Wu and his colleagues had no effective treatment for their plague patients, and almost all of them died, their enlightened use of quarantine and isolation methods proved to be critical for controlling outbreaks. Because of their work, doctors and scientists were now much better equipped to slow the spread and reduce the death toll of this deadly disease. It would be left to later researchers to finally develop effective ways to treat and even cure the plague.

CHAPTER FIVE

Plague Today and Tomorrow

Despite their groundbreaking discoveries about the cause, transmission, and control of the plague, the doctors of the third pandemic were little better equipped to treat their patients than were those of the Black Death. The real breakthrough in the treatment of plague, and all diseases caused by bacteria, came later in the twentieth century with the discovery of a new kind of drug—antibiotics. Antibiotics are chemical substances naturally produced by microbes that can kill or inhibit the activity of other microbes and cure the diseases caused by them. Their discovery revolutionized the management of infectious diseases.

The First Antibiotics

The discovery came quite by accident. In 1929 Scottish scientist Alexander Fleming was studying the bacterium *Staphylococcus aureus* (commonly called "staph"), a common and usually harmless bacterium normally found in the human body. One day he found that some of his staph cultures had become contaminated with a mold called penicillium—the same kind of mold that causes the blue-green spots on old bread. Fleming noticed that the staph bacteria would not grow near the mold spots on the culture dish. He realized that the mold must be producing a chemical that could kill the bacteria. He grew cultures of pure penicillium mold and found that it could kill several kinds of disease-causing bacteria. He realized that if the mold chemical, which he named penicillin, could be produced in large amounts, it might have a beneficial use in medicine for the treatment of bacterial infections.

In the late 1930s and early 1940s, British and American researchers worked together to develop ways to increase the production of penicillin from mold. By 1943 enough penicillin was being produced by drug companies to give to soldiers who had been wounded in the D-Day invasion during World War II, to try to prevent and treat wound infections.

Penicillin, the same blue-green mold found on bread, produces a chemical that can kill disease-causing bacteria.

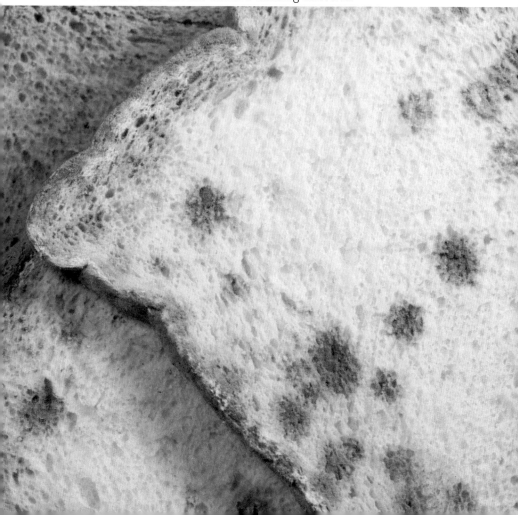

At about the same time, German scientist Gerhard Domagk published his work with another class of drugs called sulfonamides, or sulfa drugs. Sulfa drugs proved to be highly effective for treating pneumonia, meningitis, and other bacterial diseases. Sulfa drugs were also used extensively during World War II; soldiers carried containers of sulfa powder and were taught to sprinkle the powder on open wounds to prevent infection.

Bacterial Resistance

When microorganisms like bacteria are exposed repeatedly to an antibiotic, they have the ability to alter their own structure so that they become resistant to the effects of the antibiotic. Four years after penicillin was first used, scientists began seeing new strains of bacteria that had developed a resistance to penicillin, and the drug was no longer effective against them. One of the first bacteria to do this was *Staphylococcus aureus*—ironically, the very bug that had been killed by it in Alexander Fleming's lab twenty years earlier. The search was on for new antibiotics.

A Breakthrough in Plague Treatment

Unlike the discovery of penicillin, nothing was accidental about the discovery of the next major antibiotic. Selman Waksman, a microbiologist at Rutgers University in New Jersey, had for several years been studying organisms found in soil that seemed to have antibiotic properties. (Waksman is credited with actually coining the word *antibiotic*.) By 1943 he and his team had isolated a chemical from a soil organism called *Streptomyces griseus*. They called the chemical streptomycin. Testing of the new drug showed that it was effective against several kinds of bacteria—most important at the time, the bacillus that causes tuberculosis. In the late 1940s streptomycin was tried on several severe cases of plague that had not responded to treatment with penicillin. The results were remarkable. The patients felt better within hours of starting streptomycin treatment. Today, streptomycin and several other antibiotics are the first-line treatment medications for plague.

More About Antibiotics

Antibiotics are medications used to treat infections caused by bacteria. They are also often given to help prevent infections from starting, such as before certain operations. Antibiotics work in two basic ways. Bactericidal antibiotics, such as penicillin and streptomycin, kill bacteria by interfering with their internal cell functions or with the formation of their cell wall. Other antibiotics, such as tetracycline and sulfa drugs, are bacteriostatic, meaning they prevent organisms from growing and multiplying. Antibiotics are very selective; they can fight bacteria without harming the body's natural cells. Some antibiotics work against many kinds of bacteria; others work against only a few. Antibiotics do not work on any kind of virus, because viruses are not actually living cells, just fragments of genetic material.

Sometimes, antibiotics may also kill some of the "good" bacteria that normally live in the body. This may cause side effects, such as nausea or diarrhea. It can also cause the overgrowth of other normal body organisms, causing fungal infections. The throat infection called thrush is an example of a fungal infection caused by the use of antibiotics. Other side effects may include kidney stones, abnormal blood clotting, or sensitivity to sunlight. Some people have antibiotic allergies and may break out in a rash or hives or have difficulty breathing if they take them.

Bacteria that are constantly exposed to antibiotics are able to adapt over time so that they become resistant to the antibiotic. They may change their own structure or even learn how to destroy the antibiotic, and they can pass this ability on to later generations. Resistant bacteria can create serious public health problems. It is very important not to overuse antibiotics or use them incorrectly, such as for treating colds and other viral infections, because this lets bacteria adapt and become resistant to them.

Plague treatment took a huge leap forward with the development of effective antibiotics like streptomycin, but doctors desired a way to prevent people from ever getting it in the first place. They wanted a plague vaccine.

A Vaccine for Plague

A vaccine is a medicine which, when injected into a person, makes the person immune to a particular disease so that they cannot get sick from it. Vaccines exist for many illnesses, such as influenza, measles, mumps, chicken pox, smallpox, tetanus, and polio, among others. Vaccines are usually made from an attenuated, or weakened, form of the pathogen that causes the disease. They may also be made from killed pathogens. When the vaccine is injected, the body's immune system responds as if the live, active pathogen were present, and antibodies are made that attack the pathogen. Antibodies remain in the body for the rest of the person's life, keeping the immune system ready to fight off the disease if exposed to it again. An effective vaccine for plague would therefore give the immune system a "head start" and could protect millions of people who may be at risk for exposure to plague.

One of the earliest researchers in developing a vaccine for plague was Waldemar Haffkine. Like so many other renowned medical scientists, Haffkine had worked at the famous Pasteur Institute in Paris. In 1893 he developed a vaccine for cholera that proved to be invaluable for controlling a severe epidemic in India. When plague broke out in India in 1896, Haffkine set to work on a plague vaccine. At first it was somewhat successful, and he even used it on himself. Unfortunately, one of the doctors administering the vaccine to local villagers used a batch that had been contaminated with tetanus germs, and nineteen people died. Haffkine was blamed, and even though he was cleared of any wrongdoing, he lost his position in Bombay. Later, during the Manchurian epidemic of marmot plague, his nephew Paul Haffkine used his uncle's vaccine in his plague hospital. It was not very effective, and several of his staff died from pneumonic plague.

Twentieth-Century Vaccines

Since the early 1900s many more vaccines for plague were developed and tried, but none were reliably effective, especially against pneumonic plague, and they had serious side effects. In 1952 scientists developed a different kind of vaccine, called a subunit vaccine. Rather than using whole cells, a subunit vaccine uses a protein molecule found on the surface of the plague organism as an antigen to stimulate the immune system to produce antibodies. The protein they used is called F1. The F1 protein contributes to the virulence of plague because it helps the organism to interfere with the host's immune system.

Laboratory employees handle a vaccine for the bubonic plague in early 1963.

Although the vaccine made with F1 seemed to work well in test animals, it did not work against some strains of *Y. pestis* that do not happen to have the F1 protein.

Starting in the 1960s, subunit vaccines containing another plague protein, called the V protein, were developed. The V protein helps the plague organism to get into and damage the cells that it attacks. It also helps the organism resist the immune system's defenses. Like the vaccines made from F1, these vaccines were not reliably effective because there are several different varieties of V protein.

Despite their limitations, plague vaccines were given to thousands of people where plague was endemic, such as Indonesia, Madagascar, and Vietnam (where plague broke out during the war in the 1960s). Although the vaccines provided some degree of protection, none of them were considered safe or effective enough for routine use, especially in developed countries where plague is not common enough to risk the side effects. Since the terrorist attacks of September 11, 2001, however, interest in developing a reliable vaccine for plague has increased. The reason for this heightened interest is renewed concerns about an old threat—bioterrorism.

Biological Warfare and the Plague

The Mongol warriors who in 1347 launched the plague-ridden bodies of their fellow soldiers over the walls of Caffa are said to be the first ones to use disease as a weapon against their enemies. During World War II the Japanese dropped small ceramic containers containing grain with fleas infected with *Y. pestis* on cities in China. When rats came to eat the grain, they would become infested with the fleas. Several local outbreaks occurred. One survivor remembers:

I was fifteen years old at the time, and I remember everything clearly. The Japanese plane spread something that looked like smoke. A few days later we found dead rats all over the village. At the same time, people came down with high fevers and aches in the lymph nodes. Every day, people died. Crying could be heard all through the village. My mother and father—in all, eight people in my family—died. I was the only one in my family left.[35]

After the war, scientists in both the United States and the Soviet Union developed methods for aerosolizing plague, so that it could be widely spread as a mist that could be inhaled. This method eliminated the need for the flea vector. Today, several strains of *Y. pestis* are known to be resistant to the antibiotics used to treat it. Some people are concerned that these resistant strains could be used as a biological weapon to spread plague. It would be very difficult to control an outbreak of antibiotic-resistant plague, especially pneumonic plague. A safe and effective plague vaccine is especially important now because it would help to prevent such a weapon from succeeding.

New and Improved Plague Vaccines

In the late 1990s combination vaccines containing both the F1 and the V proteins together were developed by teams from the United States, England, and Canada. They worked quite well against both bubonic and pneumonic plague in test animals, and in the last ten years, testing in humans has shown it to be very promising against bubonic plague. Testing its effectiveness for pneumonic plague, however, is being done only in animals such as mice and primates (monkeys and apes). So far, the tests have shown that the combination vaccine seems to work better in some primate species than in others, so it is not yet known how well they will work against pneumonic plague in humans. Current research is studying ways to administer the vaccine safely to people. Another potential for improvement in the plague vaccine is being studied by a team of researchers at Wake Forest University in North Carolina. In 2005 they discovered that when a protein called flagellin is added to an existing plague vaccine before giving it to laboratory mice, the vaccine stimulates the mouse immune system to produce antibodies at a rate five hundred thousand times faster than without the flagellin. Flagellin is a substance found in the whiplike "tails"

A plague vaccine developed by researchers at Wake Forest University has been tested on primates without having any side effects.

that some bacteria use to move themselves around. Adding it to the vaccine protected the mice from pneumonic plague for three months. The vaccine had no bad side effects when tested on monkeys, and if it protects them from plague effectively, the scientists hope to start testing in humans. Another advantage of this vaccine is that just a few drops inhaled through the nose are enough to provide protection, and an injection is not necessary. "Flagellin can function as an effective adjuvant [addition], making a vaccine that protects against the most dangerous form of the plague—pneumonic plague," reports Dr. Stephen Mizel, professor of microbiology and the leader of the research team. "These results clearly establish a strong foundation for the future use of flagellin as an adjuvant in humans,"[36] he said.

Studying Plague Genetics

Another area of plague research involves studying the genetics of the organism. In 2001 the entire sequence of *Y. pestis* genes—its genome—was mapped. Studying the genetics of *Y. pestis* is extremely difficult because it has an uncanny ability actually to change the sequence of its own genes. It also can pick up genetic material from other bacteria and viruses and incorporate it as its own. These characteristics suggest that the plague organism has undergone a great deal of change over thousands of years. Understanding the organism's genetic structure allows scientists to understand better how the organism evolved long ago from a relatively harmless intestinal bacterium into a highly virulent and lethal organism that can live in so many different kinds of animals. It helps them learn how the plague organism can cause so much damage, especially in the lungs. It also helps them understand how it develops resistance to antibiotics and how to develop new and better ways to treat and prevent plague.

Preventing Plague

Until a safe and effective plague vaccine is perfected, steps can be taken to reduce the threat in areas where plague is endemic. The first method has to do with environmental management. This means controlling rat populations both in cities and in the countryside. In most developed nations this is not a problem. But in many poorer, underdeveloped countries, efforts at rat control may be too costly. In these areas it is especially important that health officials carefully monitor all cases of plague in both humans and rodents. The use of pesticides to control flea populations is also helpful in preventing the spread of plague.

People who live in areas where plague is endemic, such as the American Southwest, can do several things to reduce their risk of getting plague. They can make sure that no food, such as garbage or pet food, is left near their homes. Piles of brush or rocks should be removed so that rodents cannot find shelter there. Sick or dead rodents should be reported to the local public health agency so that the animal can be examined for plague infection. Pets, especially cats, should be kept free of fleas, and people should use insect repellents when outdoors to prevent flea bites. If a person suspects he or she may have been exposed to plague, either from an animal or from another person, immediate medical attention is critical so that antibiotics can be started immediately to help keep the person from getting sick.

Still a Threat

Despite the best prevention measures, plague is still endemic—existing in the bodies of rodents and other animals all the time—in many places in the world. These are the places in the world that have the greatest potential for a natural outbreak of plague. The World Health Organization reports between one thousand and three thousand cases worldwide each year, most of them in Asia and parts of Africa. In 1994 an outbreak of pneumonic plague in India killed 876 people. It had devastating

Since 2002, thousands of cases of pneumonic plague have been reported in Africa.

effects on India's economy because trade with other nations had to be stopped.

In 2002, 1,822 cases were reported in six African countries. The next year, five African countries reported 2,091 cases. In 2006 hundreds of cases of pneumonic plague were suspected in the Democratic Republic of the Congo. Madagascar, the large island that lies in the Indian Ocean near the "mouth" of Africa, reports an average of 200 to 400 cases per year, more than any other single country. Plague is still endemic in the southwestern United States, but only 7 cases were reported in 2007, 2 of them fatal.

Plague in the Future

Plague has been called a "reemerging" disease because of signs that it may be making a comeback in certain parts of the world. Several factors contribute to this trend. First is the fact that nearly 4 million rats are born every day. About ten rats exist for every human on the planet. With an ever-expanding human population, controlling the growth of the rat population, especially in cities, may become increasingly difficult.

Another factor may be climate change. Some scientists suggest that plague becomes more active following warmer springs followed by wet summers because these conditions are better for both fleas and bacteria. This may have been a factor in both the Black Death and the Asian pandemic. Norwegian scientist Nils Stenseth says, "Analysis of tree-ring climate data shows that conditions during the period of the Black Death were both warmer and increasingly wet. The same was true during the origin of the third pandemic when the climate was wetter and underwent an increasingly warm trend."[37] Some scientists are concerned that the current trend toward global warming may make conditions ripe for more outbreaks.

Stenseth and many others warn against considering plague as only a disease of the past. Plague is still around, and in spite of tremendous advances in public health, methods of diagnosis, and treatment with antibiotics, plague most likely will never be eradicated, or eliminated entirely, from Earth.

The "Plagues" of Tomorrow

As terrifying as plague has been through the centuries, today other potential "plagues" are causing great concern the world over. AIDS has killed millions of people since it first appeared in the early 1980s. About fifty-seven hundred people die from it every day. Newer diseases such Ebola virus, bird flu, SARS (severe acute respiratory syndrome), and others are emerging as potential infectious threats in the future. "We're only a jet-plane ride away from our next epidemic, and we're actually in this race with microbes," says Samuel Stanley Jr., director of the Center for Biodefense and Emerging Infectious Disease Research at Washington University, St. Louis. "They have this incredible ability to evolve, they're changing all the time, and as they change they become resistant to the antibiotics. . . . And at this point in time, I'm not sure who's winning the race, but it may not be us."[38]

In their book *The Great Plague: The Story of London's Most Deadly Year*, A. Lloyd Moote and Dorothy Moote write:

> The most dreaded disease ever to afflict humankind shares a crowded stage with infectious diseases that have not yet made their last curtain call. A wide variety of bacterial and viral pathogens have clung tenaciously to life for hundreds or thousands of years. In the seventeenth century . . . wave after wave of typhus, smallpox, dysentery, and influenza struck capital and countryside. The threats continue. The recent history of malaria, tuberculosis, and AIDS reveals reasons for maintaining vigilance against all potential microbial killers.[39]

Despite these dire predictions, great cause for hope and optimism exists, especially where plague is concerned. As plague expert Wendy Orent writes:

> Long periods of quiescence [or inactivity], in which the plague germ hides in the soil or in the reservoirs of all-but-resistant animals, are interrupted by violent outbreaks

Genes, AIDS, and the Black Death

In 1665, during the Great Plague of London, the residents of the small town of Eyam voluntarily quarantined themselves in order to prevent spread of the plague. Normally, that would have amounted to a death sentence for all who lived there. Only about half of them died, though. Could those who survived have had something in their genetics that made them better able to survive plague?

In 1996 scientists located a group of people who were descendants of the residents of Eyam and examined their genetic structure to see if they had any unique genetic characteristics in common. To their surprise, they discovered that the descendants of the Eyam survivors carried a genetic mutation called CCR5. CCR5 was already known to scientists for its ability to provide resistance to the HIV virus, the virus that causes AIDS; people who have two copies of the mutation are virtually immune to the virus. They also knew that the CCR5 mutation became much more common sometime during the 1300s, the time of the Black Death. Some scientists believe that the Black Death plague exerted selective pressure on the mutation. In other words, people with the mutation were more able to survive the plague, have children, and pass the mutation on to future generations. They feel that it is possible that the same mutation that allowed people to survive the Black Death now confers immunity to HIV to their descendents who have inherited the mutated gene.

that kill thousands of living things: this is the natural history of plague. Today, with an intense and effective global surveillance system for plague in place, and with a host of antibiotics, this natural pattern has been interrupted. Plague is still a virulent and dangerous disease, but close vigilance and effective treatment make a natural outbreak less likely than at any time in human history.[40]

Notes

Introduction: The Scourge of Mankind

1. John Kelly, *The Great Mortality: An Intimate History of the Black Death, the Most Devastating Plague of All Time*. New York: Harper Collins, 2005, p. xii.
2. Norman F. Cantor, *In the Wake of the Plague: The Black Death and the World It Made*. New York: Free Press, 2001, pp. 6–7.
3. Cantor, *In the Wake of the Plague*, p. 25.

Chapter One: What Is Plague?

4. National Institutes of Health, "Single Gene Leap Led to Flea-Borne Transmission of Plague Bacterium," news release, April 25, 2002. www.nih.gov/news/pr/apr2002/niaid-25.htm.
5. Quoted in National Institutes of Health, "Single Gene Leap."
6. Quoted in Newswise, "Bubonic Plague Kills by Cutting Off Cellular Communication," University of Michigan, September 15, 1999. www.ns.umich.edu/htdocs/releases/story.php?id=2882.

Chapter Two: The Plague in Ancient Times

7. Quoted in Ole Jorgen Benedictow, *The Black Death, 1346–1353: The Complete History*. Woodbridge, Suffolk, UK: Boydell, 2004. p. 38.
8. Quoted in William Rosen, *Justinian's Flea: Plague, Empire, and the Birth of Europe*. New York: Viking, 2007, p. 219.
9. Quoted in Rosen, *Justinian's Flea*, p. 217.
10. Procopius, *History of the Wars, Vol. II*, reprinted as "Procopius: The Plague, 542," Internet Medieval Sourcebook, Paul Halsall, ed., Fordham University Center for Medieval Studies. www.fordham.edu/halsall/source/542procopius-plague.html.

11. Procopius, *History of the Wars, Vol. II.*
12. Procopius, *History of the Wars, Vol. II.*
13. Quoted in Rosen, *Justinian's Flea*, p. 223.
14. Quoted in Rosen, *Justinian's Flea*, p. 246.
15. Procopius, *History of the Wars, Vol. II.*
16. Rosen, *Justinian's Flea*, pp. 210–11.
17. Quoted in Rosen, *Justinian's Flea*, p. 251.
18. Quoted in Rosen, *Justinian's Flea*, p. 260.

Chapter Three: The Black Death

19. Quoted in Wendy Orent, *Plague: The Mysterious Past and Terrifying Future of the World's Most Dangerous Disease.* New York: Free Press, 2004, p. 113.
20. Quoted in Orent, *Plague*, p. 115.
21. Quoted in James Cross Giblin, *When Plague Strikes: The Black Death, Smallpox, AIDS.* New York: HarperCollins, 1995, p. 20.
22. Quoted in Orent, *Plague*, p. 128.
23. Quoted in Orent, *Plague*, p. 124.
24. Kelly, *The Great Mortality*, p. 283.
25. Quoted in Orent, *Plague*, p. 155.
26. Quoted in A. Lloyd Moote and Dorothy C. Moote, *The Great Plague: The Story of London's Deadliest Year.* Baltimore: Johns Hopkins University Press, 2004, p. 259.

Chapter Four: The Third Pandemic

27. Quoted in Orent, *Plague*, p. 178.
28. Quoted in Moote, *The Great Plague*, p. 273.
29. Quoted in Moote, *The Great Plague*, p. 276.
30. Quoted in Orent, *Plague*, p. 182.
31. Quoted in PBS Online, "Bubonic Plague Hits San Francisco," *A Science Odyssey: People and Discoveries.* www.pbs.org/wgbh/aso/databank/entries/dm00bu.html.
32. Quoted in Orent, *Plague*, p. 183.
33. Quoted in Orent, *Plague*, p. 184.
34. Quoted in Orent, *Plague*, p. 184.

Chapter Five: Plague Today and Tomorrow

35. Quoted in Rebecca Bishop, "The History of Bubonic Plague," University of Texas Health Science Center at

Houston, December 2, 2003. http://dpalm.med.uth.tmc
.edu/ courses/BT2003/BTstudents2003_files%5CPlague
2003.ht.

36. Quoted in Medical News Today, "New Combination Vaccine Effective Against Plague," May 22, 2005. www.medical newstoday.com/articles/24901.php.

37. Quoted in BBC News, "Climate Linked to Plague Increase," August 22, 2006. http://news.bbc.co.uk/2/hi/science/nature/ 5271502.stm.

38. Quoted in T.J. Greaney, "Diseases Researched at New MU Laboratory," *Springfield (MO) News-Leader*, November 24, 2008, p. 5A.

39. Moote, *The Great Plague*, p. 288.

40. Orent, *Plague*, p. 5.

Glossary

acute respiratory distress syndrome (ARDS): A life-threatening complication of severe or long-term illness in which a person's lungs fill with fluid that interferes with normal breathing.

adjuvant: Any addition to a treatment method that improves the effectiveness of the treatment.

antibiotic resistance: The ability of organisms to adapt their structure so as to make antibiotics ineffective against them.

antibiotics: Medications used in the treatment and prevention of infections caused by bacteria.

antibodies: Proteins made in the immune system that attack and destroy invading organisms.

antigen: Any foreign organism or object that triggers the immune response.

arable: Agricultural term meaning land that is usable for planting crops.

autoclave: A device used for sterilizing objects.

autopsy: An examination on a deceased person to find out the cause of death.

bacilli: Bacteria shaped like tiny rods.

B cells: Specialized cells in the immune system that produce antibodies that aid in the destruction of antigens.

bacteria: Single-celled microorganisms involved in several natural processes such as digestion, infectious disease, and decay.

bactericidal: Any chemical, such as antibiotics, that kill bacteria.

bacteriostatic: Any chemical that prevents bacteria from growing and multiplying.

bioterrorism: The use of pathogens as a weapon.

bloodletting: The ancient practice of attempting to cure disease by opening a vein and allowing blood to be removed.

buboes: Large, inflamed lymph nodes seen in bubonic plague, usually in the neck, armpits, or groin.

bubonic: A form of plague characterized by the presence of buboes.

culture: A means of growing microorganisms in the laboratory so that they can be studied.

endemic: Naturally occurring at all times in a particular place, such as a disease endemic to a certain part of the world.

epidemic: A higher-than-normal number of cases of a disease.

epidemiology: The study of how illness, disease, and environment affect the health of a population.

eradicate: To completely eliminate a microorganism from existence.

flagellants: A medieval organization whose members engaged in public physical self-punishment, believing it would stop the plague.

flagellin: A chemical derived from the whiplike tails of certain bacteria which, when added to plague vaccine, seems to make it more effective.

gangrene: The death and decay of part of the body because of infection or lack of blood supply.

host: The animal on which a parasite, such as a flea, lives and feeds.

humors: In medieval medicine, one of the four major fluids of the body—blood, phlegm, black bile, and yellow bile—that determined a person's state of health.

immunity: The state of being unable to catch a certain disease, either from being vaccinated against it or from already having had it once and recovering from it.

infectious: A disease that can be transmitted from one animal or person to another.

lactic acid: A chemical produced by muscle activity or tissue destruction, normally flushed out of the body, that can build up to dangerous levels during severe disease or injuries.

leukocytes: Specialized immune system cells responsible for protecting the body from infection.

lymphatic system: The system of tissues and tiny vessels responsible for producing white cells in response to antigens and for transporting them through the body.

lymph nodes: Small glands located along lymphatic vessels, especially in the neck, armpits, and groin, that filter bacteria and other foreign substances from the body.

marmot: A large rodent, similar to groundhogs and prairie dogs.

miasma: In medieval medicine, a poisonous vapor in the air, thought to come from swamps and decaying matter, that could cause disease.

multiple organ failure: A life-threatening complication of severe illness in which several organ systems fail to function.

pandemic: A very large-scale epidemic of disease that affects a large part of the world.

parasite: Any organism that survives by feeding off another organism without providing any benefit to that organism, possibly causing illness or death.

pathogen: Any microorganism that is capable of causing illness.

penicillin: One of the first antibiotics, made from the mold *Penicillium.*

pneumonic: Relating to the lungs, and the most severe form of plague.

primates: The order of mammals that includes monkeys, apes, and humans.

reservoir: An animal that carries an organism in its body so that it can be spread to other animals.

septicemia: An infection of the bloodstream.

septic shock: A life-threatening loss of blood pressure caused by overwhelming infection.

serfs: Peasant farmers during the Middle Ages who lived and worked on their master's land in return for part of the crops they produced.

streptomycin: An antibiotic made from soil organisms that is effective against plague and other infections.

subunit vaccine: A vaccine made from certain antigens of a virus or bacterium, rather than from the entire organism.

T cells: Specialized immune system cells that search out and destroy invading pathogens.

toxin: A substance that is harmful in some way to living organisms.

vaccine: A medication made from killed or inactivated forms of a virus or bacterium that provides immunity from the disease it causes.

vector: An insect such as a flea or mosquito that carries a pathogen from one animal to another.

virulent: Capable of causing serious disease by breaking down the defense mechanisms of the infected organism.

virus: An ultramicroscopic, nonliving pathogen made up of fragments of genetic material that causes disease by multiplying itself inside other organisms.

Organizations to Contact

Center for Infectious Disease Research and Policy (CIDRAP)

University of Minnesota Academic Health Center
420 Delaware St. SE, MMC 263
Minneapolis, MN 55455
phone: (612) 626-6770
Web site: www.cidrap.umn.edu

CIDRAP provides leadership in improving public health policy and practices, promoting preparedness for emerging infectious disease and bioterrorism threats, and conducting research.

Centers for Disease Control and Prevention (CDC)

1600 Clifton Rd. NE
Atlanta, GA 30333
phone: (800) 232-4636
Web site: www.cdc.gov

A part of the Department of Health and Human Services, the CDC works to promote health in all people in all parts of the world through education, research, and monitoring of existing and emerging health threats.

National Institute of Allergy and Infectious Diseases (NIAID)

NIAID Office of Communications and Government Relations
6610 Rockledge Dr., MSC 6612
Bethesda, MD 20892-6612
phone: (866) 284-4107
Web site: www3.niaid.nih.gov

NIAID conducts and supports research on the diagnosis, prevention, and treatment of infectious, immunologic, and allergic diseases.

World Health Organization (WHO)

Regional Office for the Americas
525 Twenty-third St. NW
Washington, DC 20037
phone: (202) 974-3000
Web site: www.who.int/en

The health authority within the United Nations system, WHO is responsible for providing leadership on global health matters, supporting research, setting standards for health worldwide, providing health support to countries, and monitoring and assessing health trends.

For Further Reading

Books: Nonfiction

Holly Cefrey, *The Plague*. New York: Rosen, 2001. An easy-to-follow overview of plague focusing on the Black Death.

Fiona MacDonald, *The Plague and Medicine in the Middle Ages*. Milwaukee: World Almanac Library, 2006. The story of the Black Death in the context of medical knowledge of the time.

Charles J. Shields, *The Great Plague and the Fire of London*. Philadelphia: Chelsea House, 2002. A detailed history of two disasters that befell London, England: the Great Plague of 1665 and the Great Fire of 1666.

John Townsend, *Pox, Pus, and Plague: A History of Disease and Infection*. Chicago: Raintree, 2006. A short overview of the history of diseases, infections, and important medical discoveries from ancient times to the present.

Books: Historical Fiction

Mary Hooper, *At the Sign of the Sugared Plum*. New York: Bloomsbury, 2003. In June 1665, excited at the prospect of coming to London, teenage Hannah is unconcerned about rumors of plague until, as increasing numbers of people succumb to the disease, she and her sister Sarah find themselves trapped in the city with no means of escape. (Sequel: *Petals in the Ashes*, 2004)

Jill Paton Walsh, *A Parcel of Patterns*. New York: Farrar, Straus, and Giroux, 1983. Mall Percival tells how the plague came to her Derbyshire village of Eyam in the year 1665 and how the villagers determined to isolate themselves to prevent further spread of the disease.

Elizabeth Wein, *The Sunbird*. New York: Viking, 2004. When, in the sixth century, plague spreads from Britain to Aksum, young Telemakos travels to the kingdom's salt mines to discover the identity of the traitor who is spreading plague from port to port.

William Wise, *Nell of Branford Hall*. New York: Dial, 1999. Nell Bullen recounts the horror of the Great London Plague of 1665 and how the "Circle of Death" was drawn around her village to keep the disease from spreading to neighboring towns.

Web Sites

Centers for Disease Control and Prevention (www.cdc .gov). Searchable Web site provided by the Centers for Disease Control and Prevention for information on many health topics.

Directors of Health Promotion and Education (DHPE): "Plague Facts" (www.dhpe.org/infect/plague.html). The DHPE was founded in 1946 to strengthen, promote, and enhance public health education nationally and within state health departments.

Diseases from Animals (www.diseasesfromanimals.org). A site that focuses on diseases that can be transmitted to people from animals.

Medicine Net (www.medicinenet.com/script/main/hp.asp). Searchable site for information on health-related topics.

Wrong Diagnosis.com (www.wrongdiagnosis.com). Part of the Health Grades network, this site provides information on a multitude of health and illness topics.

Index

Picture Credits

About the Author

Lizabeth Hardman received her bachelor of science degree in nursing from the University of Florida in 1978 and her bachelor of science degree in secondary education from Southwest Missouri State University in 1991. She currently works full-time as a surgical nurse.

Hardman has published both fiction and nonfiction for children and adults. She especially enjoys writing about medicine and history. She lives in Springfield, Missouri, with her two daughters, Rebecca and Wendy, three dogs, two cats, and two birds. When she is not working or writing, she enjoys reading and hiking and is a fan of the St. Louis Cardinals and the Florida Gators.